LIGHT YEAR '86

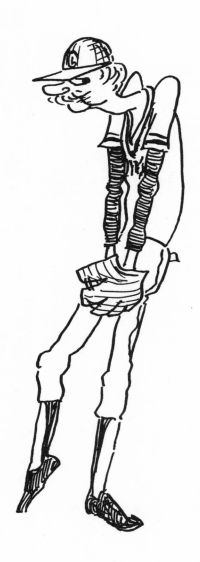

LIGHT YEAR
'86

Edited by Robert Wallace
With drawings by Leonard Trawick

Bits Press
Cleveland

The acknowledgments on pages 275-276 constitute a
continuation of this copyright notice.

Associate editors: C. M. Seidler, Bonnie Jacobson.

Printed and bound in the U.S.A.

ISBN: 0-933248-04-0
ISSN: 0743-913X

Light Year, the annual of light verse and funny poems,
welcomes submissions. Poems recently published in
periodicals are OK. SASE, please. To:

> Bits Press
> Department of English
> Case Western Reserve University
> Cleveland, Ohio 44106

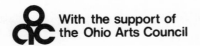 With the support of
the Ohio Arts Council

Who are a little wise, the best fools be.
                                    John Donne

There was a naughty boy
    And a naughty boy was he,
He kept little fishes
    In washing tubs three . . .
                                    John Keats

CONTENTS

1

THE GIFT OF THE MAGI

The angel of the Lord sang low
and shucked his golden slippers off
and stretched his wings as if to show
their starlit shadow on the wall
and did the old soft shoe, yeah,
did the buck and wing.

The Magi put their arms around
each other, then with chorus-line
precision and enormous zest
they kicked for Jesus onetwothree
high as any Christmas tree
and Caspar was the best.

And Melchior told a story that
had Joseph sighing in the hay
while holy Mary rolled her eyes
and Jesus smiling where He lay
as if He understood, Lord,
knew the joke was good.

But Balthazar began to weep
foreseeing all the scenes to come:
the Child upon a darker stage
the star, their spotlight, stuttering out—
then shook his head, smiled, and sang
louder than before.

There was no dignity that night:
the shepherds slapped their sheepish knees
and tasted too much of the grape
that solaces our sober earth
O blessèd be our mirth, hey!
Blessèd be our mirth!

Peter Meinke

MR. JONES DODGES THE BULLET

Someone just fired a gun in Zanzibar
and the bullet is headed your way, says Mrs. Jones.

Really, dear, says Mr. Jones,
that is hard to believe.
He leans over to pet the cat.

Woo, says Mrs. Jones, that was a close one.

Andrew J. Grossman

ONLY THE SHADOW KNOWS

When the shadow of an airplane goes across a prairie
And the groundhog looks up to see if it's spring
And can't see his own shadow because of the airplane,
How do the meteorologists call it?
Beyond the shadow of a doubt, only the shadow knows.
When Peruvian airforce pilots enjoy the shadows of
        complex structures
Such as a railroad bridge in the Andes
With a small stream thousands of feet below washing its
        thousands of
Trestled feet and
An old steam engine puffing across the top
Like a spider ice-skating across his silk bridge
With hundreds of sacks of flour to deliver,
What is it good for?
Only the shadow knows.
When a thin man stands sideways in the sun
Does his bulging shadow express his gluttonous nature?

Shadows can not goof off by themselves.
They are completely subservient to this world.
Each ass cheek has its parallel in the other,
Each object in this logical universe has its parallel in its
        shadow.
In shadows, is it also survival of the fittest?
Do shadows jog so as to be more competitive when they
        try out for
Shadow plays in Czechoslovakia in the autumn?
When George Washington was crossing the Delaware
What did his shadow think about crossing at night
And being left out of the glory?

Kirby Olson

THE RAVEN REVISITED

Once upon a midnight bleary, from TV both weak and
        weary,
After hearing "Where's the beef?" so many times that I
        could snore—
While I nodded, nearly napping, suddenly there came a
        tapping,
As of someone gently rapping, rapping at my condo door.
" 'Tis a neighbor being mugged," thought I, "who's
        rapping at my door—
                Only this and nothing more."

Presently I sank in slumber and was truly sawing lumber
'Til, methought, a storm-tossed barbecue bounced off the
      sliding door.
As my hand reached out to check it, something black
      reached in to peck it,
And I cried out, "What the heck?" It was a Raven on my
      floor—
A most stately Raven, such as Poe once wrote of, on my
      floor.
          "Out!" I said, and nothing more.

Though we once had let the stork in, this occasion called
      for Orkin.
Pausing not, I grabbed the phone as through the Red
      Book I did leaf.
But my fingers stopped their walking when the Raven
      started squawking,
For, in fact, the bird was talking as I stared in disbelief—
And one statement did it issue as I stared in disbelief.
          Quoth the Raven, "Where's the beef?"

"Bird," said I, "who sounds so trendy, be thou sent by
      Hell or Wendy's?
Dost thou fly about the city filling other chains with
      grief?
Art thou pet to Clara Peller, trained by Sedelmaier to tell
      her
When to mug it up and sell her line so catchy yet so
      brief?
Is it thou who prompts the lady who found fame with
      line so brief?"
          Quoth the Raven, "Where's the beef?"

Scott Fivelson

AT SUNOCO, THEY ALSO SERVE

Attendants watch the figures jump,
idle while the driver works the pump.

Robert Wallace

ON SHOVELLING THE DRIVEWAY AND
OTHER JOYS OF SINGLE-FAMILY DWELLING

Let me live in a condo beside the road,
    With time for fun undivided—
Do-it-yourself on a permanent shelf,
    And underground parking provided!

Virginia Killough

REFLECTIONS

I mean, cats can't get at fish, hate getting wet.
Fish can't get at worms, hate getting dry.
        He moved his pole a mite.
If cats had a taste for worms, be more fish.

*

Used to know a man in Dubuque, Iowa.
   Used to sit on the courthouse steps.
Asked him once what he was doing.
      He said:
      Drinking whiskey and spitting out the seeds.

Daniel J. Langton

THE NAKED TRUTH

News item: Beauty queen dethroned when it becomes known that she
   had once posed for nude magazine photographs.

Now see the queen on throne repose
Until some wagging tongues expose
That she once posed without her clothes
   And hadn't told.

They said the costume that she wore
Had naught behind nor more before.
It was a costume to deplore.
   And rather cold.

They thought it moral turpitude
That she'd been pictured in the nude.
The price of candid pulchritude:
   Some people blush.

So here's a queen without a throne,
A queen who's had her cover blown,
Because some prude had known she'd shown
   A royal flush.

Robert N. Feinstein

YET MORE BRATS

Down the blowhole of a whale
Mal poured ice-cold ginger ale.
"Ha!" he chuckled, "there she blows
Tickly bubbles out her nose!"

All at once, two vast tail-slaps
Caused his sailboat to collapse.
After several months the Coast Guard
Dropped Mal's folks a "no luck" postcard.

(Whales are docile beasts unless
Forced to fizz and effervesce.)

*

At the laundromat Liz Meyer
Flung her brothers in the dryer.
Round and round they've whizzed for years,
Not yet dry behind the ears.

*

On the dam Neil spied a wheel
That seemed to whisper, "Twist me, Neil!"
Neil thought, "Sure, why not?"—which urge
Caused Las Vegas to submerge.

*

While the fruit boils, Mom sends Lars
Out to hunt for jelly jars.
In the twinkling of an eye
Back he bounds with a supply:
Jars in which old Doc McBones
Used to keep folks' kidney stones.
"Lars, you darling!" Mother cries.
"These look perfect! Just the size!"

Only those with steely nerves
Taste Mom's stoneless peach preserves.

*

By the dark shores of Loch Ness
Christine gathered watercress
Thus defying common sense.
Something slimy and immense
Munched her, and (what's more distressing)
Took its salad without dressing.

*

Dirty Bertram, that is who,
Filled Dad's beer mug with shampoo
Giving Dad himself instead
Of his beer a foaming head.

*

Paul, in Aunt Pru's prune surprise,
Plunked two artificial eyes.
Uncle, seeing when he stirred
Someone stare without a word,
Wondered: "How come what Pru cooks
Always gives me glassy looks?"

*

Through the fishtank glass (SMASH! BANG!)
Hurtled Howard's boomerang.
Circling round the room it creamed
Mother's cut-glass vase.
                              Dad beamed.
"That's right, Howard! That's the thing!
Growing boys should have their fling!"

*

Into Mother's slide trombone
Liz let fall her ice cream cone.
Now when marching, Mother drips
Melting notes and chocolate chips.

*

With the garden sprinkler Brett
Drenched the television set
Just to find out: Will flash floods
Turn soap opera to suds?

*

In a glacier Horace Hind
Made a monumental find:
A pair of lizard-looking knees
Locked tight in ice for centuries!

Zoologists beheld with awe
That whole live thing begin to thaw.
Why, who'd've thought an allyosaurus
Would still have teeth to sink in Horace?

*

With her one-string ukelele
Mona drives her Dad mad daily,
Twanging songs of just one note.
Say, what's that jammed down Mona's throat?

X. J. Kennedy

NO SPACE FOR TIME

I cannot wear my pocket watch,
But I refuse to hock it;
Unlike today, tomorrow may
Bring back the old watch pocket!

Ned Pastor

LINES WRITTEN IN ANSWER TO A QUESTION POSED BY A VICTORIAN DOMESTIC POET

O Moon, when I gaze on thy beautiful face,
Careering along through the boundaries of space,
The thought has often come into my mind
If I ever shall see thy glorious behind.

—lines reportedly discovered by Sir Edmund Gosse and
attributed by him to a "housemaid poet"

O Moon, when I saw thee careering past,
With Apollo on TV I saw thy behind:
It was like thy face from plaster cast
But none the less glorious to my mind.

William Jay Smith

BARSOOM

It breaks
over me like
a wave of
cold water &
I put the
book aside
& look at
myself:
beer gut, small-boned wrists,
& spindly legs,
wondering
just what
in the hell
I'm doing
beneath the moons
of Mars
slashing the
lifeblood out of
Tharks.

John Bell

PRAGMATIST

Apocalypse soon
Coming our way
Ground zero at noon
Halve a nice day.

Edmund Conti

AFTER OPENING THE STATE OF CALIFORNIA 1983 INDIVIDUAL INCOME TAX FORM 540

"Revenue and Taxation Code Section 19417 provides for a $500 penalty for filing a frivolous return."

Frivolous? I was prepared to be honest,
well, discreetly honest. You know what I mean.
I'm afraid to begin. Tempt me and I'm easy
as grass. "Don't touch that empty socket,"
my mother said when I was five. For two days
I held out. On the third I urged
one slow finger toward the nippled copper prong.
In my refrigerator
I stock raw carrots, unsalted tuna, Kosher dills,
Cottage cheese. Nothing I can't say *no* to.
Because I can't say *no*: to lobster
stuffed with its own tomalley, artichoke
hearts smothered in Hollandaise, cherry tarte
flambé, another glass of the $30 cabernet sauvignon.
Give me a choice and I'll take both
butter and sour cream on my baked potato.
Now this word *frivolous* who
cached it among the Basic English
of the State of California Franchise Tax Board?
It disconcerts. Like a funeral guest
dancing a soft shoe at the open grave.
The sky is grim
and there's the sound of earth on the coffin,
but today, today we're alive.
I'll buy opulent colored inks, violet
and pistachio, sign my name in Gothic,
fold the form so daffodil petals fall into his hand.
Surely white falcons, three

of them, flying from Sacramento
on alternate noons, will deliver my refund
in coins of new-minted silver.

Sally Croft

FLOWER POWER AT LAST

In the American countryside there is a low moan of
     anti-business.
Cows wake *giving*. Rabbits abandon their offices, lie on
     their backs in the sun.
Tommy abandons *his* office in the city, hurries back on
     the 2:17,
takes off his shoes, chats with himself like a schoolboy.
Inevitably, though, he is overheard by a daisy.
The daisy is upwardly mobile, dreams of an office
in the city, of trading with Tommy.
Accordingly they trade.

The next day the daisy sits at Tommy's desk, goes to
      lunch with his secretary.
Tommy meanwhile lies sprawling in the hayfield.
In mid-afternoon he falls asleep, dreams he is back at
      work, then
wakens to find the field full of former executives.
They are lying thick on the ground, like slugs.
A secretary hen crosses her drumsticks
and takes corporate dictation, from a zinnia in a four-in-
      hand.

Frederic Will

OH, OH

My girl and I amble a country lane,
moo cows chomping daisies, our own
sweet saliva green with grass stems.
"Look, look," she says at the crossing,
"the choo-choo's light is on." And sure
enough, right smack dab in the middle
of maple dappled summer sunlight
is the lit headlight—so funny.
An arm waves to us from the black window.
We wave gaily to the arm. "When I hear
trains at night I dream of being president,"
I say dreamily. "And me first lady," she
says loyally. So when the last boxcars,
named after wonderful, faraway places,
and the caboose chuckle by we look
eagerly to the road ahead. And there,
poised and growling, are fifty Hell's Angels.

William Hathaway

ROVER BEACH

(For Dick and Paula Jesson)

The doggy-doo is thick to-night.
My stomach, too, is full, and Rover seems
To have the trots;—On the Clam Shack the bug bulb
Flickers and is gone; the lakefront, shimmering, stands
Glimmering and swimmering. Litter strews the sand.
Close the windows, foul is the night air!
Cockers, poodles, sheep-dogs and the like despoil the land.
Listen! you hear the grating roar
Of people floundering in the muck who find
A dry spot, and returning up the strand,
Begin, and cease, and then again begin
To sink with tremulous cadence slow
Up to their knees in residue.

Sophocles long ago
Put his foot in it by the Agean
And it brought to mind the misery
Of Philoctetes, Oedipus,
The fetid ebb and flow
Of bad luck and the idea of catharsis.

It reminds me
Of my girlfriend. Thelma Wapshingle.
She, too, was at the full and round and soft,
But she deserted me
One moon-blanched night for Izzy Obermann,
The Scholar-Gipsy.

Ah, me! I find eternal sadness in
The breath of the night-wind as it wafts o'er,
For it stirs visions vast and drear
Of starry eyes and mossy haunts
And naked Wapshingles of the world.

Ah, Duck, let us be true
To one another! for the beach which seems
To lie before us like a murky stew,
Putrid, miserable, and full of doggy-doo,
Hath neither joy, nor love, nor light,
Nor music, alcohol, nor colours bright,
Nor funny stories, birds, nor peace of mind,
Nor girls, nor pleasant scenery of any kind.
And we are here on crapulous Rover Beach,
Swept with yowls and confusing fog,
As vicious animals are unleashed
And life goes to the dogs.

Michael Hinden

MORE RIVER RHYMES

Drifting down the Amazon
With the tops of my pajamas on,
I hit a rock and all asunder went—
I fear some people glimpsed my fundament!

*

As I was sailing on the Baltic
I found my watch did not at all tick,
I thought, one way to make it run'll
Be to bang it on the gunwale.

*

When I was on the River Dee,
A jolly miller sang to me:
"I care for nobody, no not I . . ."
A psychopath! I sailed on by.

*

Sailing on the River Don
I questioned my translator, Olga:
"How come no '*ay yuch nem*' sung?"
"Oh, *that* song is for the Volga."

*

Drifting on the golden Yangtze,
Dolled up for the girls to see me;
I like to, with the girls, be handy,
For I'm a Yangtze dude all dandy!

*

Sailing through the Land O' Lakes
I heard the helmsman mutter,
"This water's hard to navigate—
It's all clogged up with butter!"

*

When we were sailing on the Pee Dee
We queued up at a lock—not speedy;
I fumed, "Whatever can we do
To leave this river P. D. Q?"

*

Drifting down the River Liffey
I was getting rather squiffy;
When you drink you should stay *chez maison*—
I had drunk a quart of Jameson.

*

Sailing down the stately Rhine,
I heard some singing, "Auld Lang Syne"—
I turned my back, for I am moral, I
Will not hearken to *Die Lorelei!*

*

It was floodtime on the Seine:
Flotsam, jetsam, garbage, then
Five cats clinging to a plank—
Un, deux, trois cats sank!

William Cole

DINNER WITH THE ROCKEFELLERS

Taking a bath together before we go
down for dinner, thus passing the buttock
school of tapestry, I think that perhaps
after all I can do without
my next wife, the Japanese masseuse,
for you are soaping me quite ably
and from the murmurations left and right
I think that's what's going on
in the other *appartamenti*, redheads
on both sides (like Beatrice Cenci).
In these big villas, high among the cypress trees,
they attend to most details, tea
twice a day brought on trays, but walls
are paper-thin. That is, perhaps,
their way of keeping folks
on their best behavior, treading
quietly, speaking softly, soaping
not too loudly. To celebrate,

moving down the long hall dressed in tux,
I break a stalk off, put in my lapel
a great yellow crysanthemum, and dare
the Duchess herself to ask me
where I got it, or the florid smile
that makes confession non-essential.
Tonight it's Crema Orientale and as usual
I'm passing up the fine liqueurs
on the silver tray that's trundled past.

David Ray

THE HOUSE PARTY

We were invited to a house party last weekend in Lake
        Forest, Illinois, which I shall not soon
forget, and this is not only because I brought what turned
        out to not be the right clothes for it,
but, more objectively, the people were alarming at best.
When I got up in the middle of Friday night there were
        lots of the guests
running through the hall and leaping in and out of each
        other's rooms together,
who mercifully didn't see me. I had to call them all
by their first names except Mrs. Farley, even though I
        shall never see any of them again,
such as Davenport and Davis, Manfred, Ritzinda, Conall
        and Yvette.
I remarked to Davenport when we were playing croquet
        that my second son at the age of three had cleverly
        been wont

to refer to croquet mallets as golf hammers, at which
        Davenport laughed not at all;
yet, to be fair, realizing that he had been less than
        sympathetic, he very kindly told me
the plot of the Thorne Smith he had been reading the
        previous night, although I bet that's not all he was
        doing.
Davenport confided to me over several pousse-cafés that
        he is a grain arbitrator,
and then Manfred (one of the world's worst names) came
        along and we talked about grain.
Usually I like to talk to men but it was difficult to talk to
        these ones
or difficult for them to talk to me at any rate, but that
        was OK
because it transpired that the women talked together a
        great deal in little pockets.
Ritzinda true to *her* name wore a dress that had only one
        shoulder and not much of that on Saturday for
        dinner.
Mrs. Farley told me I should put apricot oil on my face a
        little at a time and it would be absolutely
        wonderful,
much the way Davenport had talked about grain,
        although I certainly don't think Mrs. Farley was in
        the apricot oil business.
Ritzinda of the single shoulder asked me who I'd gotten
        to get me invited,
and looked somewhat addled when I said that a cousin of
        a college classmate of Yvette's had been my
        brother's piano teacher
and that some of these shared the same cleaning woman
        in Georgetown,
which is all perfectly true, if boring. Mrs. Farley
may possibly be a hundred and goes around completely
        covered with Liberty scarves,

and as one might expect there was dancing Saturday
        night well into Sunday
at which she excelled, scarves and all, and it turned out
        she had known the violinist as a young man.
Some of the other things we talked about were Carl
        Rogers, shallots, bargello,
tobacco barns, curare, giving people *la question* during the
        French Revolution and after,
encaustics of the tobacco barns, which are Yvette's idea of
        lares et penates,
David Riesman, James Agee, and exchange students in
        the Philippines.
Mason, to whom I am married and whose job is teaching
        church law to seminarians for a living and with
        whom I went to this house party,
and who incidentally got the better of the deal, can't
        figure out why I'm being so disagreeable,
inasmuch as *he* spent the whole weekend in the study
        with a marvelous and very complete collection of
        church law books
dating back incredibly far in their original bindings, and
        reading practically all of them,
and showing up for meals and cocktails during which he
        explained to Emery and Rosfrith Van de Sand
the complete history of church law, which if they had
        been going to seminary would have cost them
hundreds and hundreds of dollars, and they didn't even
        have to buy the texts,
although the Van de Sands probably couldn't have gotten
        admitted to seminary anyway
even if they'd wanted to; but of that they will doubtless
        remain forever unaware.

Caroline Knox

MARKING TIME

The door is locked, the keys within,
Left in the pocket of yesterday's pants.
I have my Walkman, I might dance—
But I'd rather share my chagrin.
No doubt *you*'ve done the same dumb thing
Sometime. No need to feel disgraced;
Keys are so easily misplaced.
Try not to fret. You must find something
Constructive to do, like read, or sift
The garbage for a crossword puzzle.
Already my thoughts begin to drift.
If I do have a beer, I must not guzzle.
Who knows how long I'll have to wait?
Please, God, don't let Charlie come home late!

Tom Disch

A SIMPLE DEFINITION OF INTERMARRIAGE

Intermarriage is the lawful union
of a dissimilar man and woman
(providing these dissimilarities
fall within one or more categories
the defining society uses such as
hue, nationality, religion and caste,
matrilineally, patrilineally, or both,
wherever applicable unless unknown).

(Note: In cases of consanguinity
change "dissimilar" to "similar.")

Perhaps an example would be
helpful: If a white Lutheran
cocktail waitress from Brooklyn
running for Congress
on the Republican ticket
marries a Jewish Ethiopian prime minister,
regardless of whether they graduated Harvard together,
it is intermarriage
(unless the cocktail waitress
wins the state lottery prompting
her long-lost half-
black father
to phone, and the Ethiopian army
stages a coup,
the prime minister escaping to Brooklyn—
with diamonds in his toga
equal to the lottery after taxes—
where,
having established his three-year residency

and proved his fluency
in English, he may or may not
vote the straight Republican ticket
providing the cocktail waitress's
mother is Jewish).

(Note: Should the cocktail waitress
lose the election
and the couple leave on an extended vacation,
include all local criteria,
particularly if the prime minister
perisists in wearing his toga.)

(Of course, if the prime minister
is the long-lost father's son
it is intermarriage consanguinal
except where prohibited by law.)

Bonnie Jacobson

ROOMS

There are rooms to start up in
Rooms to start out in
Rooms to start over in
Rooms to lie in
Rooms to lie about in
Rooms to be lied to about being lied about in
Rooms to lay away in
Rooms to lay up in
Rooms to lay over in
Rooms to lie low in
Rooms to lie about being laid up in
Rooms to be put in
Rooms to be put up in
Rooms to be put up to in
Rooms to be put up with in
Rooms to be put up with for putting on in
Rooms to put down in for putting up with being put off
      in putting forth in
Rooms to turn in in
Rooms to be turned in in
Rooms to be turned on in
Rooms to be turned down in
Rooms to be turned around in
Rooms to be turned over in
Rooms to be overturned in
Rooms to turn away in when being held off in
Rooms to be turned upon in for turning up turned out in
Rooms to hold back in
Rooms to hold in in
Rooms to hold out in
Rooms to hold on in
Rooms to hold forth on in about being held off in

Rooms to be held down in
Rooms to be upheld in
Rooms to withhold in when being held up in
Rooms to sit up in
Rooms to sit down in
Rooms to be set down in
Rooms to sit about in
Rooms to set about in
Rooms to set out in
Rooms to sit in on in
Rooms to be set aside in
Rooms to be set upon in
Rooms to sit up in to be set off in
Rooms to be set back in for sitting out in
Rooms to be set up in for being sat on in for sitting back
      in
Rooms to be upset in
Rooms to give in
Rooms to give in in
Rooms to take in in
Rooms to be taken in in
Rooms to be mistaken in
Rooms to be mistaken about in
Rooms to take over in
Rooms to be overtaken in
Rooms to take up with in
Rooms to be taken up on in
Rooms to give in in about being taken up in
Rooms to give over to being taken on in
Rooms to be taken off on in for being taken aback in
     about being given away in
Rooms to give up in

Ray Griffith

JAPANESE FISH

Have you ever eaten a luchu? It's poisonous like fugu, but it's cheaper and you cook it yourself.

You cut it into little squares as fast as possible but without touching the poison-gland. But first, you get all the thrill you can out of the fact that you're going to do it. You sit around for hours with your closest friends, drinking and telling long nostalgicky stories. You make toasts. You pick up your knives and sing a little song entitled "We who are about to dice a luchu." And then you begin.

George Starbuck

FOOD

It is always there,
Man's *real* best friend.
It never bites back;
it is already dead.
It never tells us we are lousy lovers
or asks us for an interview.
It simply begs, *Take me*;
it cries out, *I'm yours.*
Mush me all up, it says;
Whatever is you, is pure.

John Updike

INNARDS

As many ripples,
loops and fingers,
kinks and pockets,
scallops,
curls and ruches
as the surf
on frilly waves—
      corrugated, convoluted
      slippery links and
      pinks and puckers,
      frothy overlapping
      fringes:
            Enormous
            Anemone!
            Look
            in the Anatomy Book:
            the spastic heap
            indented, redundant,
            crimped, voracious,
            over-abundant,
                  squeezing,
                  mashing,
                  munching,
                  pinching,
                  spitting
                        it out. The end?
                        No, still more
                        clench and squirm
                        and fretted froufrou
                        at each bend:
                              a bore,
                              the belly
                              a bushel

of tripe. I turn
to the velvet kidney,
the orderly heart,
liver and lungs' aesthetic
pattern. They somewhat
soothe the gripe.
But it's hypnotic,
that exotic page.
Could I unravel
      the capacious maze,
      the conduit of travel,
      my future might
      come clear.
            It says here,
            that *if*
            I could uncoil,
            could straighten
            it, I'd have a thong—
            What would I do with it?—
            28 feet long.

May Swenson

ROOT CANAL

under the anesthetic
tiny gondoliers
sing to me

pizzicato
and I am
borne away

helpless as
childhood
as they pole

through the shadowed
waters
of the mouth

Linda Pastan

THE RUN

There goes the shot and the muddle of runners,
there go the slips of their black license numbers.
There go their breaths and the back of their shorts,
there go the dogs and invalid sorts,
    with death in the rear, all bony and glum,
    walloping slow on a black bass drum.

Now are the loudspeakers taking a snooze
and the friends of the runners waiting for news.
Now are the dots on the domino-timer
flashing in numerals higher and higher,
    as the sun like a medal hangs in the cold,
    blank in its alloy of silver and gold.

Here come the runners in patches like fog—
cheekbone and nipple, wheelchair and dog.
Here come the lenses twisting themselves
for finish-line pictures to put up on shelves,
    with death in the front, all bony and spry,
    fiddling a jig at the powder-blue sky.

Mark McCloskey

RANDOLPH SCOTT IS SEVENTY – NINE TODAY

I never quite understood your appeal.
You were, to me, boring.
Rather monk-like, the face "craggy";
your shirts were tunics, buttoned diagonally,
your hats had strings that met
under the chin, making them bonnets.
Whenever you raised the bonnet,
to Joanne Dru or Dorothy Malone or Ruth Roman—was
        it?—
it made one gasp with disappointment to see
your sparse hair, its recruit cut.
We never knew you. You never let us in.
You were the monk with the gun. The chaste kisser.
Scott, we never saw your tongue!
We remember the names of none of your horses.
And you will surely not have stuffed
your best steed, unlike the bestial Roy.
And yet you shot straight, rode tall,
stood up to the bad ones, manfully.
Yet, somehow, you were memorable.

Today you are seventy-nine, and visiting
the Mayo Clinic, south of us, for a check-up.
You must be frail now, the temples
all veins. I hope at home you do not
count out your hours in some sunless canyon.
I hope in your dreams you are not always cantering
into plywood towns. I hope you do not spend
evenings behind drawn shades, painting your toe-nails.
I hope you wear no kind of diaper.
Does Joanne ever call? Do you hear from Dorothy?
Could that be Ruth at the door, having done

something clever with raspberries?
Who's taking care of you? *Is* there someone?

If they're not good to you at the Mayo,
not expert, deferential, awed maybe,
let us know. But somehow I'm confident
that you are looking out for yourself,
even now, while wheeled among medications,
toward unspeakable procedures—will they ever
be done?—confident that you still
sit tall, that you never take crap from anyone.

Michael Dennis Browne

2

ENTROPIC VILLANELLE

Things break down in different ways.
   The odds say croupiers will win.
We can't, for that, omit their praise.

I have had heartburn several days,
   And it's ten years since I've been thin.
Things break down in different ways.

Green is the lea and smooth as baize
   Where witless sheep crop jessamine
(We can't, for that, omit their praise),

And meanwhile melanomas graze
   Upon the meadows of the skin
(Things break down in different ways).

Though apples spoil, and meat decays,
   And teeth erode like aspirin,
We can't, for that, omit their praise.

The odds still favor croupiers,
   But give the wheel another spin.
Things break down in different ways:
We can't, for that, omit their praise.

Tom Disch

SLIM PICKINGS

All we had for breakfast was bread—
but it was very good bread.

All we had for lunch was crackers—
but they were very good crackers.

All we had for dinner was buns—
but they were very good buns.

All we had next morning was crumbs—
but they were very good crumbs.

James Steel Smith

ON FIRST LOOKING INTO MRS. BEETON'S ALL ABOUT COOKERY, A COLLECTION OF PRACTICAL RECIPES, LONDON, 1874

Mrs. Beeton in the cold rain
Thinks of Mr. Beeton in his coffin,
The bills she can't pay,
And October's "Dinner for 18 Persons"—
Mock turtle soup, removed by:
Crimped Cod and Oyster Sauce;
Soles à la Normandie, Red Mullet,
Julienne Soup, removed by:
John Pory and Dutch Sauce.

Mrs. Beeton sees this for October,
For 18 persons in October,

The leaves still slipping from the trees,
Nostalgia of summer and death everywhere.
Mr. Beeton cold in the grave,
Mrs. Beeton, nose running,
Sniffs and thinks of Entrées:
Sweetbreads and Tomato Sauce,
Oyster Patties (Faint chime of bells,
Recalling the Crimped Cod, memories),
Stewed Mushrooms, Fricandeau de Veau and
Celery Sauce.

Falling rain, the leaves dead on the street,
Mrs. Beeton smiles at the rain, the leaves,
And at the Second Course:
Roast Saddle of Mutton, Grouse Pie, Ham,
Larded Turkey, Roast Goose, Boiled Fowls and
(Ring the changes!)
Oyster Sauce.

Mrs. Beeton chortles at the golden rain,
The flaming leaves, October rubiat, victorious,
And at the Third Course:
Pheasants removed by Cabinet Pudding!
Custards, Gâteau de Pommes, Lobster Salad,
Prawns, Compôte of Plums, Apple Tart, Italian Cream,
Peach Jelly and Roast Hare removed by:
Iced Pudding.

"There, that's better!" says Mrs. Beeton,
Savouring the bright October fields
And the calves, hares, oysters, cod, puddings
All grazing so happily in the October sun
And there, replete, refulgent,
Mr. Beeton, ascending.

Charles Squier

PUTTING A NAME ON IT

My friend Bill the doctor
lives in South America,
where he once saved the life
of an Amazon Indian child,
whose grateful parents
added "Bill" to the name
the little fellow had already.
If each of us took the names
of those who had saved us,
why, my own name would be so long
that no one could remember it.
And naturally I would like to think
one or two people out there
might have my name
trailing after theirs
like a shy, reliable friend.

The problem is this:
as the world grew more
and more beholden, each of us
would take all
of each other's names,
and soon everyone would be
called Tom Edna George Muhammed
Aloysius Eileen Jose,
and in the end we would be crushed
by these huge names.
Personal income would plummet.
Whole nations would starve.
We wouldn't have time for anything
except Name Maintenance

unless, of course, we all took
the one name of David,

perhaps shortening it
to "Dave" for the sake of brevity
and to hasten world peace:
the headline would say,
"Dave Meets Dave in Geneva;
World War III Postponed Indefinitely."
Epictetus says everything
has two handles,
one by which it may be borne
and one by which it may not.
I say send me your tired,
your worn, your cumbersome name,
which doesn't work anyway.
I have this new one for you.
Some monosyllable!
In Hebrew it means "beloved."

David Kirby

LADY DI AND I

Lady Di is pregnant
With another royal tot.
Glory, glory hallelujah—
Am I glad that I am not!

L. C. Dancer

SKIN DEEP

The liquefaction of the clothes
portrayed in *Vogue* conveys a hint:
whether in silks my Julia goes
or nearly nude, it costs a mint.

Marian Gleason

TOP MODEL GIVES INTERVIEW

Fine thigh, fine breasts, fine brow. Thoughts mean and
    canned.
Poor little she-ape at the Steinway grand.

John Frederick Nims

SYMPATHY

See her face a mask of powder,
conceive her heart a blown rose—
not the crone in cast-off clothes
a shopping bag on both elbows—
the starlet on the tabloid cover.

Celebrity isn't just a pose,
as the poor success would have you think.
She's never free to take a drink
or fool around with a friendly wink,
for every indiscretion shows.

So far this month we've seen her sink—
an innocent who'd put her trust
in a beachcombing Romeo gone bust—
then rise, in the mini-series *Lust*,
from a negligent look to a mink.

For her future the stars predict dust
to dust in the usual ways: cocaine,
custody suits, walks in the rain,
running off a curve high on champagne,
reliving vanished glories dawn to dusk.

All of it makes you feel the pain
the famous feel. It feels fine:
but then you're just standing in line,
comparing your juice with their wine.
It's a raw deal all around in the check-out lane.

Dan Campion

THE GODDESS

I have seen the goddess
with my mortal eyes they

were filming down the
street and it was Meryl

Streep she was attended
by five trailers eight

trucks thirty technici-
ans and four policemen

the whole street was il-
lumined with a heavenly

blaze she walked up the
steps of the house four

times and I know that she
saw me and smiled at me

she knew that I was her
devotee she went into

the house and they said
the next scene was in-

side and I couldn't go
in will I ever see her

again my goddess but it
doesn't really matter I

saw her and she knew me.

James Laughlin

ROSES KEPT FALLING
ALL OVER AMHERST

My grandmother's gone now
but for 14 years
she shared the earth with Emily Dickinson
for 24 years
with the Little Flower of Jesus
and for 25 with me

Sometimes at night
when I think I'm sleeping
the four of us
gather in Emily's kitchen
(its walls still
apple-green and yellow)

Emily's wearing her white dress
(the one that now hangs
in her bedroom closet
covered with the dry cleaner's
pristine plastic)

She serves us sherry
(the color of her eyes)
and black cake
(her own recipe)
telling us it calls for 19 eggs

Of course
she talks about her father
while I try not
to talk about mine

Thérèse is wearing her Carmelite habit
carries her roses
in a Monoprix shopping bag

Her red Renault
is parked at the curb

I ask her what it's like
being the Little Flower of Jesus
Does she really go around
showering roses?

            My grandmother's wearing
            the green voile dress
            she bought in the summer of '44

            She tells Emily and Thérèse
            they're the smart ones—
            never getting married

That she still wishes
she hadn't

I ask where would I be
if *that* had happened?

She swaps gingerbread recipes with Emily
asks Thérèse if she knew how to cook

I tell them
when I was 14
I read *The Story of a Soul*
"A Narrow Fellow in the Grass"
and
Gone With the Wind

and wanted to be

       a nun
       a poet
       in bed with Rhett Butler

(not necessarily in that order)

Thérèse drops a rose petal
into the sherry

       Granny says
       we should have invited
       Margaret Mitchell
       "But she won't leave Atlanta
       Hangs around Peachtree Street
       even in bad weather"

Emily says she met Rhett once
in the tall grass at Twelve Oaks
just before Scarlett
started throwing the crockery

Granny starts drinking
her third glass of sherry
(Since her death
I guess
she's quit being a Baptist)

We reminisce about how
the year that Emily was called back
Thérèse was called to be a nun

How in my grandmother's lifetime
Thérèse was born
               died
               declared a saint

How when I was 14
Harvard College bought Emily's manuscripts
"But I kept them from getting
my white dress"

               I tell them how
               when I was 16
               I planned to be

                         a poet
                         a nun
                         a saint
                         good in bed

          (not necessarily in that order)

Emily smiles and slices some black cake

Thérèse says she did well
at the second and third

My grandmother keeps quiet

Roses plink on the roof
like rain

Jeanne Shannon

MAD ABOUT THE GIRL

"Yeats loved great big women. He would have been mad about Vanessa
Redgrave."

—Rebecca West

Vanessa Redgrave, meet William Butler Yeats:
He's here by benefit of séance.
His heart, his heart—oh, how it palpitates!
He's seen your films, of course, though in a trance.

Your Julia—how it made him want to sing.
Your Isadora made him want to dance.
An aged man, though he's a paltry thing,
Stands here, most passionate of fans.

Edward Watkins

ODE TO H.D.

Hilda Doolittle
did a lot.
Hilda Doolittle
will not be forgot.
But the question is:
Hilda Doolittle did what?

Rudy Albers

JOE GOULD'S SONG

Easter time is coming,
the geese are hanging high;
please put your hand upon
an old man's thigh.

If you haven't got a hand free,
your upper lip will do;
if you haven't got an upper lip,
then God bless you!

And if you've got a harelip,
your husband is a hound;
tell him what I just told you
the other way around.

G. N. Gabbard

POSSUMMA

for William Harmon

These things are real, children:
Who needs to make things up?

Invocation

"O possum,"
you apostrophize to the pet-sized specimen
slumped in the headlights of your old Nova,
                the '63 Oxymoron,
"if, as a hick once joked in a movie,
            the state animal of Mississippi
is a dead dog in the middle of the road,
I nominate you, O most ancient of days,
              for national mascot!"

*

The Manifest Witness of History

1. American

At precisely
mid-millennium, Senor Pinzon, envious chief
of the Niña, presents a New World *didelphis*
              to his dubious patrons,
Ferdinand and Isabella. The court murmurs
          as their majesties poke their fingers
     in its pouch. *Zarigüeya!* They are delighted!
In Jamestown a century later, Captain Smith,
             new Adam in pantaloons,

             interrogates the Indians
for native names to give the animals.
"And this?" "Ugh—possum," growls the chief.

"O-possum!" proclaims
Smith to his scribe, fixing the vestigial vowel.
"Animal mirabile," his brethren
scratch in their diaries by candlelight,
"with an head like a Swine, a taile like a Rat,
& of the bignes of a Cat."

Further on, M. LaSalle,
at the heart of the midwestern wilderness
later to claim his name for a de-luxe model
with wings and whitewalls,
encounters a pair of *rats du bois* in the bushes
and dispatches them with his baton.
Soon he swaggers back to camp, possums slung
from his belt. *"Voila!"* he cries. *"Tableau!"* thinks
his artist, title ready:

"LaSalle at the Portage."
If only Franklin had known the possum's pedigree,
150 million years, more venerable than even
his beloved turkey!
Would the Congressional delegates have voted it
a place on the Great Seal, clutching
thirteen arrows in its prehensile tail
and persimmon branches in each foot, *possumus,*
e pluribus unum?

2. Literary

Consider: why did Eliot,
fastidious Anglo-Catholic, Royalist, lapsed Yankee,
call himself Old Possum? And would he have been able,
Blessed Gabriel Rossetti,
to keep a less likely Pre-Raphaelite pet
than the possum that slept on his table?

3. Natural

"Nature amazes me," as someone summed up
a workshop-worn poem. That the possum is called
                    "living fossil"—cousin

                    to wombat and bandicoot,
contemporary with gingko tree or horseshoe crab,
the mammals' ace white-haired knuckleballer
                    in the World Series
of evolution—is curious enough. But the male
                    sports an anatomical feature,
          stranger than fiction, stranger than the fact
of the female's dozen-day gestation, that firmly
                    clinches the prize.

          It's simply this:
the possum has a forked penis, a by-God genuine
twi-night doubleheader. This gave rise to the rumor
                    of a nosy pioneer
that possums mated through the lady's snout
                    and that, after incubation in the sinus,
          the missus sneezed the measly naked litter
into her pouch—yet another triumph of fecundity
                    over intelligence.

                    *

Benediction

          When McPhee wrote, "Be
a possum is the message, and you might outlive God,"
he had the species in mind, not pea-brained heroes
                    trying to scramble to
the other, greener side of suburban autobahns.
                    The last thing your late possum heard
          was rubber thunder behind headlights' lightning,

then a bald four-part descant, some EAT MORE POSSUM
pickup fading away.

Now he balloons
for the ants' Thanksgiving parade, a memento mori
grinning from the road's cold shoulder. If only he
could shake this swoon
for a final wish, it might be what any body asks:
to play himself again, to resurrect
blinking from the rotten ditch, to shuffle
across the way toward some immortal shade and climb
into the sky to sleep.

Michael McFee

ODE

In this epoch of high-pressure selling
    When the salesman gives us no rest,
And even Governments are yelling
    "Our Brand is Better than Best";
When the hoardings announce a new diet
    To take all our odor away,
Or a medicine to keep the kids quiet,
    Or a belt that will give us S.A.,
Or a soap to wash shirts in a minute,
    One wonders, at times, I'm afraid,
If there is one word of truth in it,
    And how much the writers were paid.

O is there a technique to praise the
    HOTEL GEORGE WASHINGTON then,
That doesn't resemble the ways the
    Really professional men
Convince a two hundred pound matron
    She's the feather she was in her youth?
Well, considering who is the patron,
    I think I shall stick to the truth.
It stands on the Isle of Manhattan
    Not far from the Lexington line,
And although it's démodé to fatten,
    There's a ballroom where parties may dine.

The walls look unlikely to crumble
    And although, to be perfectly fair,
A few entomologists grumble
    That bugs are exceedingly rare,
The Normal Man life is so rich in
    Will not be disgusted, perhaps,
To learn that there's food in the kitchen,
    And that water comes out of the taps,

That the sheets are not covered with toffee,
    And I think he may safely assume
That he won't find a fish in his coffee
    Or a very large snake in his room.

While the curious student may study
    All the sorts and conditions of men,
And distinguish the Bore from the Buddy,
    And the Fowl from the Broody Old Hen;
And presently learn to discover
    How one looks when one's deeply in debt,
And which one is in search of a lover
    And which one is in need of a vet;
And among all these Mrs. and Mr.'s,
    To detect as each couple arrives,
How many are really their sisters,
    And how many are simply their wives.

But now let me add in conclusion
    Just one little personal remark;
Though I know that the Self's an illusion,
    And that words leave us all in the dark,
That we're serious medical cases
    If we think that we think that we know,
Yet I've stayed in hotels in most places
    Where my passport permits me to go
(Excluding the British Dominions
    And Turkey and U.S.S.R.),
And this one, in my humble opinion's
    The nicest I've been in so far.

To the Manager of the George Washington Hotel
Mr. Donald Neville-Willing
and to all the staff with gratitude
and good wishes from
W. H. Auden
1939

ROBOTICA

A robot with lofty inflection
Read Stein in the poetry section,
But read it "Arose
Is arose is arose"
And thought it concerned resurrection.

*

The robotical judge never knew
Which ethical dictum was true:
"To forgive is divine"
Or "Vengeance is mine."
So he simply rotated the two.

*

A robot who reckons up rows
Of numbers with infinite O's
Regards Charles Babbage
As just an old cabbage
Who counted on fingers and toes.

*

An old robot thought it was hell
That he was unable to tell
How feeble he got,
Since it was his lot
To be terminal even when well.

*

A macro-computer designed
For tasks of a general kind,
Was courting a skinny
Young micro– named Mini,
Who dumped him as too unrefined.

*

A surgical robot named Clyde
As Med students probed him inside
And dismantled a part
Of his fiberglass heart,
Sat up and announced, "I just died."

Gloria A. Maxson

MUAMMAR EL ____?

Newsweek starts his name with K,
Time begins with G;
The New York *Times* prefers a Q,
And this bemuses me.
The Wall Street *Journal* used a K,
Then switched to Q, but why?
Perhaps it suits the ending
That was changed from y to i.
Two middle letters, d and f,
Don't add much to the fun
Until you see them doubled up—
Two for the price of one!
Then there's the matter of the h,
A letter some install
In several different places—
But others not at all!
If I were Libya's leader,
I'd fret about my fame:
Not over what they say so much
As how they spell my name!

Ned Pastor

THE HOUSEFLY

Lit on the
Aquila
Tip of the
Emperor's
Non moscas
Nose and rubbed
Hands over
Captat
Majesty.

Ernest Kroll

GENEALOGICAL QUERY

Do the Syon House dogs
who ate of Henry VIII
have descendants yet?

Does the mole whose hole
killed William III
have mole kin still?

Neither *Burke's* nor *Debrett's* knows.*

Anne Marple

---

* Henry's body was taken from London to Windsor. During a tea break at Syon House, it is said, the dogs savaged the corpse.
William of Orange died as the result of a fall when his horse stepped in a mole hole at Hampton Court. Thereafter, the Jacobites toasted "the little gentleman in black velvet."
Debrett's and *Burke's* are the who's-who of royalty, nobility, and landed gentry.

OH, LORD, TENNYSON

[Tennyson's] ordinary conversation with young ladies was likely to run on paleontology—gigantic ferns and ichthyosaurs—or on the nervous systems of lower animals."

—J. W. Beach, *The Concept of Nature in Nineteenth Century English Poetry*, p. 415.

They cluster round in two and threes
A-twitter with ecstatic pleas
To hear one line on love or fate
From the lyric lips of the Laureate.

But after how-de-do he turns
To talk of old gigantic ferns;
And, worse, the lovely things he bores
With facts concerning ichthyosaurs
And a lower animal's nervous system
When he ought to have simply up and kissed 'em.

Louis Hasley

IMAGINARY DIALOGUES

Said Marcia Brown to Carlos Baker,
"I can't get salt from this saltshaker!"
"Just try turning it upside down!"
Said Carlos Baker to Marcia Brown.

*

Said Ogden Nash to Phyllis McGinley,
"I like my ham sliced rather thinly."
"I'd slice it for you, but I must dash!"
Said Phyllis McGinley to Ogden Nash.

*

Said Dorothy Hughes to Helen Hocking,
"I can't for the life of me get on this stocking!"
"Would it help if you first removed your shoes?"
Said Helen Hocking to Dorothy Hughes.

William Jay Smith

SPORT COUPE

Young Edmund Clerihew,
This prototype of yours is too
Aston-ish, to put the matter gently.
I must ask that it not be called a Bentley.

George Starbuck

CLERIHEWS

Geoffrey Chaucer
never drank from a cup and saucer,
but that's no cause for mockery;
he lived before the age of genteel crockery.

Dean Jonathan Swift
was often miffed,
but had he been politer
he might have worn a mitre.

Emily Brontë
was seldom jaunty.
Nothing strange about that,
with a graveyard and a moor for habitat.

Vonna Adrian

Charles Lamb
Didn't give a damn
About fame.
He wrote under another name.

Louis Phillips

Empress Josephine
Liked *haute cuisine*,
But to save simoleons
She just ate Napoleon's.

Sir James George Frazer
Wore a Cambridge blazer;
He referred to his chow
As "The Golden Bough-Wow."

Margaret Blaker

Was William Butler Yeats
Fond of dates?
Did he have a passion for cheese soufflé?
His poems do not say.

William Jay Smith

HOW SWEET THE SOUND

Mr. Zane ----
And Lady Jane ----
Were, in rather different ways,
Amazing Greys.

Edmund Conti

CLASSICAL CLERIHEW

Zeus
was a goose
to think that Leda would be turned on
by a swan.

Tom Riley

THE GOD

I have no use
for Zeus.
He'd slay
to get his way
and change his shape
to rape
and I'm sure any error
he'd blame on Hera.

Lillian Morrison

INTIMATIONS OF IMMORTALITY

> And they turned once more into men,
> younger than they had been
> and taller for the eye to behold and
> handsomer by far.
>
> *Odyssey* 10.395-6

Medea was leaning over her pot. "Let's see,
what goes in with the old boy? Rosemary, at least,
and thyme and any old green I can find, only something's

wrong. Looks and smells good enough to eat, but if stew
were what I wanted I'd make stew." She called
over the fence to Thetis: "How you coming?" "Oh, not so

good. Only one came out half way decent is Achilles,
and he's defective. Gorgeous to look at, but he'll
die, just like any old mortal son or husband."

Medea said: "I'm going to have to try it on the kiddies.
If you can stand the treatment, it's *good* for you.
If it doesn't work, Jason's going to give me hell."

What young goddesses have to go through with their
         faulty connections!
I know, too, some people tell these stories all wrong.
But wasn't it really Circe? Pigged, unpigged, and better

than new, but she couldn't marry them all, and the only
one she'd have taken was afraid of what she might do to
         him.
All he wanted was to get back to his wife, who would live

like him, who would die like him. Like sensible people.

Richmond Lattimore

LOT'S WIFE

Something told me the girls had left the stove on;
I just turned back to see.

They've all gone on without me,
bickering about whose fault it was.

I tell you it's a blessed relief—
best vacation I've had in years.

Barbara D. Holender

MARQUETTE LISZT

A rollercoaster full of nuns! loukoum! ogees!
Maverick pleasance elicited Kefauver in fee simple.

"Mother, I am going to marry Lord Dumbello. Mother,
may I have a new water silk?"
Sylvan plaints, crass attitudes, vermeil, red millet.
Nike grips fungo bat; perivale resonates.

Nary of these I renounce, as pontiffs from time to time
are fettered in their proper cosmologies; nary, I say,
obviating thoughts which have whilom whilom occurred
        to Jean Genêt,
    Kierkegaard, Schopenhauer, and Ecclesiastes.

Caroline Knox

CALVIN vs. ARMINIUS

A Scots Presbyterian named Taylor
Thought Predestination a failure:
    He lived out his life
    Bereft of a wife
'Cause the Lord had forgotten to mail her.

Not so, said the Lord to Taylor,
Let's reconsider this failure;
    To wed you must woo,
    The wind that I blew
Had need of a sail and a sailor.

John Hoad

CANDIDE'S WEEDS

Whose weeds these are you bet I know;
But though I spade and rake and hoe
And try to make OUR garden grow,
The Devil's got the Vigoro.

I tell them work will cure our ills,
But Pangloss puffs, Paquette pops pills,
And Cuny cries and sighs, '*Mañana!*'
And rolls a joint of marijuana.

The old one snorts and sniffs cocaine,
'A little something for the pain,'
She says, 'to ease these almost endless days.'
The Friar free-bases, then he prays.

While all our plans go up in smoke,
On gage and hash and coke I choke.
How fast weeds grow! One seed to SEEDS!
Out, out; chop, chop; take that, you weeds.

James Camp

CALLING

A gunsmith named Samuel Baker
Was asked by his young wife, a Quaker,
    To find a new line.
    But he said, "Adeline,
I feel I should be a piece maker."

Hubert E. Hix

KNEE INJURIES BRING MEDICAL ADVANCES

> Prolonged kneeling can result in tendinitis.
>
> *(News Item)*

I pray you do not bend the knee
climbing up those heavenly stairs
to whatever gods may be.

That joint was not made cleverly
except for animals in their lairs:
four legs put less stress on the knee.

Orthopedists all agree
it's harmful when you say your prayers
to whatever gods may be.

Saints and athletes frequently
suffer traumas unawares:
I pray you do not bend the knee.

Four ligaments hold the joint, you see:
God help you if a ligament tears
(or whatever gods may be).

Surgeons artificially
can replace it—still, beware!
I pray you do not bend the knee
to whatever gods may be.

Edward Watkins

IDEALISM

A philosopher, one Bishop Berkeley,
Remarked, metaphysically, darkly,
That what we don't see
Cannot possibly be,
And the rest's altogether unlarkly.*

Ashley Montagu

* BBC pronunciation.

AFTER FIVE BOTTLES OF BEER ON THE
FRONT PORCH I'VE ABOUT DECIDED THAT
IT IS ALL GOD'S FAULT

God and I sip beer
on the front porch
while beautiful women
pass by in the street.

God says, "So you've
about decided that
it's all my fault
you can't have every
woman you want."

Suddenly I realize
that God knows what
I am thinking,
so I reach into the
cooler for that last
cold beer.

But God's hand
is there first.
He snaps off the bottle
cap with his teeth,
drains the bottle dry
and belches thunder.

I try not to think
what I am thinking.
God just laughs.
"Listen," he says,
"you're right:
ain't nobody nowhere
ruder than me."

Stephen E. Smith

SPRING COMES TO THE ARCHBISHOP

Spring comes to the
archbishop, part of it
through the sleeves and
part of it through the
bottom of his cassock

Kay Ryan

3

PROGRAMMING DOWN ON THE FARM

As all those with computers know,
Input-output is called I/O.
But farmers using these machines
See special letters on their screens.
So when they list a chicken fence
To "Egg Insurance and Expense,"
Into what file would it go?
Of course to EIE I/O.

Michael Spence

THE LOCH NESS ZUCCHINI

The Loch Ness Zucchini lies glossy in the larder.
Must quit estivating and think about hibernating
in an Olympic hurry, after to have diddled in the dooryard
(the ablative absolute, which English only approximates)

relating and all to the relatives and tennis geezers
eating Welsh Rabbit, harking to the English horn
on French leave from the Holy Roman Empire,
while the ready chinchilla kitkin mulls and slumbers on
        its stomach.

Fanatic femme, yours truly yields your project
to the complexion of whose driveway the decades have
        been disagreeable
(who logs the stupendous? what is called color in music),
        benign
Member of the Medieval Academy of America
and Students for a Democratic Society and the
        Wadawanuck Club.

Caroline Knox

HAIKU

Persimmon:
the cashier weighs
the ladybug too

Alexis Rotella

SONG OF THE CAULIFLOWER

Oh Tomato, my Tomato
Come endive with me, my sweet.
Lettuce dance the hot potato
To the avocado beet.

Don't be melon-choly, honey-
Dew you think that I yam dumb?
Bean so long since I've bean sunny
'Cause your love's cucumbersome.

Be my vegetable lover,
Oh I wish you'd come to Caul.
Here's a garden to discover.
You don't seem to carrot all.

J. Patrick Lewis

FOR THE LOVE OF BROCCOLI

My wife's got this thing about broccoli
She owns a broccoli monopoly
She'd hold the pass at Thermopoly
All for the love of broccoli.

So I asked the King of Asparagus
If there was anything that I could do.
He said, "For your sake and the rest of us,
Fix her some broccoli stew!"

Henry Rowe

DARWINIAN GARDEN

In a Darwinian garden nothing grows
Except what knows how to survive.

Here daisies thrive and ever-widening
Vines of dewberry. Self-seeded

Parsley carpets yards of earth
In patterns modelled on the Persian,

And chives and scallions thickly thrive
Like grass become gargantuan.

Descendants of once-planted snips
Of mint and cast-off violets

Defend themselves from extirpation:
Uprooted, still they multiply.

Wild roses, raspberries and black-eyed
Susans suddenly appear

And then are welcomed back each year
By one who with a reckless care

May weed or reap but does not plant,
Who at each evolutionary

Turn of earth takes time to make
A practically natural selection.

Mildred J. Nash

DICHOTOMOUS

The sparkling white
   Of the snowflakes I love'll
Cause less delight
   When the time comes to shovel.

Dorothy Sands Beers

LILAC ELEGY

Lushly grows the lilac
Where the outhouse stood.

Wilbur Throssell

SPRING

Bees to the flowers, flies to shit.

Howard Nemerov

THE GREEN BABY

There is a
       green baby sitting
at a green table
a jade face and hair
the silver spoon is green
the tablecloth green
and all the air about him
shadow green
Ailanthus green
he is eating peas

Elizabeth Eddy

FLOSSIE

Flossie is a pancake
Just a-flippin' in the pan.
We say, "Flossie, are you happy?"
She says, "I am, I am, I am!"

"I'll be golden brown in just a sec,
So I'm flippin' every chance I get.
Why, I'll break the world's record yet,
Yes sir, yes m'am, you bet, you bet!"

We say, "Wait, you're just a pancake, Flossie
Flippin' in the pan.
Are you sure you're really happy?"
She says, "I am, I am, I am!"

Henry Rowe

WHEN NANCY LIVED ON CHESTNUT STREET

When Nancy lived on Chestnut Street
There was always someone new to meet.
Six cats to greet you at the door
And wicker baskets on the floor.

On the outside stairs a cake would cool,
Angel food or macaroon.
Each visit was indeed a treat
When Nancy lived on Chestnut Street.

There were birds in cages and dogs to tease
And you could sit just where you pleased.
Lush plants grew on every sill,
Each one with its own ant hill.

Now Nancy has another house,
And her cats catch every mouse.
But life seemed somehow very sweet
When Nancy lived on Chestnut Street.

Virginia Muldoon

DIGGING TO CHINA

You're digging to China, but you stop when Louis Homer
     yells.
He says Mr. Quist's cocker spaniel's having pups.
In the garage where everyone can see them, he yells.
They comes out slick as spit, he yells.

Louis is right. There are six black ones
and one brown one. The black ones get licked up first.

The brown one is never licked all over and it's smaller.
After Louis wonders aloud if he should pick it up,

you suggest a weenie roast.
Yes, he says, you get the weenies, I'll get the matches,
meet me behind Bullock's at the haystack
and don't forget the sticks, he says.

Louis has his weenie on end to end.
You have yours stuck through the middle.
Louis has a bigger knot on the end of his weenie.
It doesn't take yours as long to ooze.

You blow on yours. Louis eats his hot.
The haystack is on fire. It's running up the curtains
of its sides the way fire does when a movie saloon's ablaze
and John Wayne has just socked a villain

who has just hit John with a chair.
And the firetruck's longer than Eddie Dubonny's garbage
        truck.
It says Gothenburg Fire Dept. in snaky gold letters on the
        door,
and its hoses suddenly jump tight.

The whole lot is black.
Your mother tells a fireman she should take a stick to you.
Louis says you set the fire, he got the weenies.
You say Louis set the fire and you got the weenies.

Louis's mom runs home to check her weenies.
Your mom says wait till your dad gets home.
Your dad has this hair brush with raised Gothic initials
(years later you'll say he only used it when he felt
        medieval).

But when he finally hits your butt, red characters issue
        from your mouth,
and in the middle of it all you know he's saying
you can't go out anymore that night,
and so you're lying there, thinking of that liar Louis,

and you know it's late because sombody's turned the
        locusts off
and your pillow's dry, and then you're dreaming.
You're dreaming the hole you dug to China's slowly
        closing,
when suddenly, Jolene Booker, the neighbor girl is there,

and her mouth's wide open, and she's yelling, but there's
        no sound in the dream.
Her mouth's just a hole under a little blonde moustache,
a hole lined with cutworms, and way back there there's a
        pink nail,
hanging like a lantern in a Chinese basement.

Don Welch

ELECTRIC BLANKET MISFORTUNE

Stupid little Lucy Wankett
Washed her automatic blanket
While the thing was still plugged in.
Notify her next of kin.

Josh Kennedy

TWINS

On the corner, the Twin Brothers grocery,
one brother in front, another in back;
when we had guests I went there for deli:
I'd order from Sam, who would say he was Jack.

Over the Jell-O with sliced bananas
they'd smile and see what they had in stock;
I had, they said, the nicest manners
and was the quietest boy on the block.

My order filled, I'd say "so long"
and wave to Jack, who would say he was Sam:
I never knew if I was right or wrong,
but I'd close the door so it didn't slam.

Edward Watkins

ATTILA THE HEN

Years after school has faded to a stack
of dust-fringed yearbooks on a closet shelf,
the dream returns to drag the truant back
by one delinquent ear. You find yourself

in class. You're either naked, or your name's
been called to give the answer. There she stands:
the teardrop glasses with the rhinestone frames,
a metal ruler flashing in her hands.

Robert Bess

GIRLS' HEADS BENT ON TAKING A TEST

Front rows
Bubble of maple, Apple butter
Coxcomb, Cobweb
Teal, Oatmeal
Vixen, Flaxen
Silver sieve, Black Olive
Maraschino cherry, Gooseberry
Yellow pompom, Marshmallow

Middle rows
Tobacco boll, Orange roll, Charcoal
Sienna clay, Ice soignée, Straw soufflé
Copper dipper, Sevenupper, Chili pepper
Honeyball, Taffypull, Waterfall
Nutmeg, Eggnog, Coconut
  Cinnamon bark, Meadowlark
  Mink mouton, Pink cotton

Rear rows
Bird's nest, Everest
Meringue caffeine, Tangerine
Peat umber, Wheat amber
Zebra streak, Mozambique
Croissant, Bon bon
Cider rain, Champagne
Gingerale, Pigtail

A. L. Lazarus

MOTHERHOOD

Teenagers borrow the car,
Toddlers play in the muck,
And—the unappealing truth—
Little infants suck.

Esther M. Leiper

ADULT NURSERY RHYME

Polly Popper,
brought up proper,
kept her uppers
in a glass,
hung her skirt
upon a fencepost,
lest she stain it
on the grass.

Judson Jerome

SOME LIMERICKS

A Matron well known in Montclair
Was never quite sure what to wear.
   Once when very uncertain
   She put on a lace curtain
And ran a bell-cord through her hair.

*

There was an Old Person who said,
Pointing out the oil lamp on his head:
   "It perhaps does not pay
   During most of the day,
But it's helpful when reading in bed!"

*

A Lady whose name was Miss Hartley
Understood most things only partly.
   When they said: "Get this straight,"
   She said: "What? —What? —What? —WAIT!"
So they had to give up with Miss Hartley.

*

A Captain, retired from the Navy,
Lived on mashed potatoes and gravy.
   He stood with an oar
   And stared at the floor,
Reflecting at length on the Navy.

*

There was a Young Man on a plain
Who wandered about in the rain.
   He said: "Well, what OF it?
   I LOVE it! I LOVE it!"
And he said so again and again.

William Jay Smith

GHOSTS

When a ghost
goes past a post,
I see the post
through the ghost.

When a captain's ghost,
sails down the coast,
I see the coast
through the ghost.

When a ghost
eats toast,
I see the toast
inside the ghost.

James Steel Smith

ANATOMICALLY SPEAKING

I'm wary of putting my foot in my mouth,
And shaking a leg just fatigues me;
Whenever I dare to stick my neck out,
The consequence never intrigues me.
I can't seem to keep a stiff upper lip,
And my eye for detail's very weak;
Now you know why I tend to play it by ear
And converse with my tongue in cheek!

Ned Pastor

THE COMMON GOOSE

The common goose converts to geese
Each time it reproduces,
But if a mongoose should increase,
Somehow it's then mongooses.

Robert N. Feinstein

KNOWING MY PLACE

I think I may
Be one of the few
Who say 'instead'
Instead of 'in lieu.'

Edmund Conti

GUESTS

Some cause happiness with their smile,
Some by being deft,
Some by being right on time,
Some by having left.

Charles Lee

COUNSEL

When the deed's done, and those events
You warned would be the consequence
Stand horridly exposed and plain,
If you would keep your friends, refrain
From speaking words they won't forgive
However long ye both shall live.
When there's no help for the afflicted
Remind them not what you predicted;
Stop at your lips the tempting phrase
That spelled the error of their ways;
Oh never, never, never quote
The words you spoke, the words you wrote.
Although it blister you, forego
The ruinous phrase "I told you so."

Sara Henderson Hay

OLD SAYING

there is a saying that goes
"you can pick your friends
and you can pick your nose
but you can't pick
your friend's nose."
errors in judgment such as this
have probably started every
major war in this century.

Samuel P. Schraeger

PARKING METER

The dial is a robber-red.
When you insert
the franc piece
in its side-lips,
twist its ear
to make it listen:
you need to leave
something in its watch.
And all of a sudden
it's awake—
ticking up to say:
I agree,
I only stand
and wait for thee.

Alamgir Hashmi

SONG FOR WOMANKIND

(A Bass Solo)

Oh, women are winsome and women are nice
But women are hard to define.
They've something in common with whales and mice
And something in common with beggarlice
And something in common with wine.

Oh, the way of a woman is subtle and sweet
And they don't have to learn it in schools.
Oh, the way of a woman is hard to defeat,
They've something in common with birdies that tweet
And something in common with mules.

Mildred Luton

RAINED OUT

To save much for a rainy day
  Is surely wise and nifty;
Every time I start it, though,
  The rain comes down like sixty.

Pier Munn

DIRTY POOL

for Truffaut

Throwing a dog
Who doesn't like water
Into the water
Is like hitting someone
You supposedly love
Once you've done it
They'll never trust you again
And the first chance they get
They'll put the bite on you
You dirty son of a bitch

Daniel Thompson

A FABLE IN TWO LANGUAGES

1. L'Oiseau, la Souris et le Chat

Un petit oiseau chantait
Sous le soleil de mai—
"Qu'il fait beau, qu'il fait beau, fait beau!"
Une souris lui chuchota,
"Ne sais-tu pas que le chat
Cherche par ici, par là,
Un morceau tendre comme toi?
Les petits diovent se taire. C'est la loi!"
L'oiseau chanta encore plus haut—
"Qu'il fait beau, qu'il fait beau, fait beau!"
Un jour vint le chat et mangea
Notre ami l'oiseau. Voilà,
Plus de chansons dans les champs,
On n'entend que le clac-clac des dents.
Et puis le chat prit la souris
Malgré les bons conseils soumis;
Il la mangea, c'est bien dommage,
Bien qu'elle fût silencieuse et sage.
La leçon qu'on apprend—qu'est-ce que c'est?
Qui ne chante jamais, ne chantera jamais.

2. The Bird, the Mouse and the Cat

A little bird warbled away,
Gay in the sunlight of May—
"What a day, what a day, day, day!"
"Psst!" hissed a mouse. "Keep it low!
Mister Pussy's out prowling, you know.
He's quite keen of hearing, and oh!
How morsels like you make him drool.
The small must keep still. That's the rule."

The bird sang still louder, "Hooray!
What a day, what a day, day, day!"
One morning, along came the cat
And caught our friend bird. That was that.
A muffled chomp-chomp, and done!
No more songs in the sun.
And next the cat ate—it's not nice—
Despite all its careful advice,
The mouse—popped it into the hopper,
Though so perfectly silent and proper.
The lesson you'll learn, if you're clever?
If you don't ever sing, you won't ever.

C. W. Pratt

THE ANIMALS' BREAKFAST

Every morning at six Tilton got up and fed the dog,
    three cats,
        the cow,
            and a Shetland pony.
But one Monday morning he slept past six,
    past seven,
        past eight.
At eight fifteen all the animals—
    the dog,
        the three cats,
            the cow,
               and the Shetland pony—

came into the house
    and lined up at the foot of Tilton's bed,
and—each in its own way—demanded breakfast:
    bow-wow,
        meow-meow,
            moo,
                and neigh-h-h!

Tilton woke up.

And the dog
    and the three cats
        and the cow
            and the Shetland pony
                got their breakfast.

James Steel Smith

LYING TO THE DOG

Tomorrow I'm going to go get
a bunch of steaks and hamburger
so you won't have to eat that
nasty dry dog food anymore.
And then we'll buy a house in
the country where you can
run around without a leash—
or better yet, how about the seashore?
Miles and miles of sand,
I know you'll love it.
And you can sleep on my bed tonight,
under the covers if you would like.
In the morning, I'll take you
for a ride in the car and you can

sit in the front seat and stick
your head out the window.
And if we make it home in time,
I'll let you bite the mailman.

Charles West

ENTER DARK STRANGER

In "Shane," when Jack Palance first appears,
a stray cur takes one look and slinks away
on tiptoes, able, we understand, to recognize
something truly dark. So it seems when we
appear, crunching through the woods. A robin
cocks her head, then hops off,
ready to fly like hell and leave us the worm.
A chipmunk, peering out from his hole beneath
a maple root, crash dives when he hears
our step. The alarm sounds everywhere. Squirrels,
finches, butterflies flee for their lives. Imagine
a snail picking up the hems of his shell
and hauling ass for cover. He's studied carnivores,
seen the menu, noticed the escargots.

But forget Palance, who would have murdered Alabama
just for fun. Think of Karloff's monster,
full of lonely love but too hideous
to bear; or Kong, bereft with Fay Wray
shrieking in his hand: the flies buzz our heads
like angry biplanes, and the ants hoist pitchforks
to march on our ankles as we watch the burgher's
        daughter
bob downstream in a ring of daisies.

William Trowbridge

GOLIATH

I found him clicking by a concrete wall,
as clumsy as a wind-up dime store jig
with one lopsided wheel. He was as big
as a pet turtle. When he'd try to crawl
up the smooth masonry, he'd always spill
back on his armor-plated top, to lie
obtuse beneath a vast expanse of sky,
waving his six black thorny limbs until,
upright, he'd try again. As beetles go,
Goliath is the largest, but his size
exposes him to scrutiny from eyes
that may be less than friendly, and although
formidable, he's quite a target too,
for any well aimed stone, or any shoe.

Robert Bess

TICK

Ruddy bloodbody
a-wriggle like a star,
why do we crush you,
as hard as you are?

Why do we loathe you,
plucked like a grape,
besotted and gray,
from Fido's fur nape?

Some creatures devour,
some burrow within;
you hitchhike and sip.
Is this such a sin?

To live is to borrow;
your interest is small.
What could be more modest?
Not living at all.

John Updike

INCREDIBLE EDIBLES

Who in his right mind could have dreamed
That crabs might make a tidbit steamed?
That lobsters with those ugly claws
Could salivate a gourmet's jaws?
Take clams and oysters, it's surprising
That one might think them appetizing.
The strange, unearthly shrimp we serve—
Who pioneered these odd hors d'oeuvres?
The thing most puzzling about seafood
Is how the darned stuff came to be food.

Bern Sharfman

DINNER FOR THREE

I fixed myself a tasty stew
and then sat down alone to eat.
When I was only halfway through,
a thin roach pranced upon my meat.

"Hey, that meat's mine! Get off!" I said.
Before I flipped it with my knife,
another nibbled at my bread:
it might have been the first one's wife.

I made my move to snuff them out
forever with a deadly crunch,
but stopped. A voice (God's voice, no doubt),
said, "Every creature needs a lunch."

And, after all, why should I scorn
two connoisseurs at my full plate?
It wasn't their fault they were born
as roaches, so we sat and ate.

Gene Fehler

THE CLAM AT BAY

I sing of the clam, the ineffable clam,
Whose abode is the floor of the bay.
The clam is a succulent morsel of food,
He never is quarrelsome, seldom is rude,
And often has nothing to say.

The clam lives a life that has not been explored
By students of sexual practice.

His behavior's so modest, retiring and such,
That, regardless how curious, not very much
Is known about just what his act is.

But something must happen, down under the sand,
Where one clam knows the sex of another,
For, whatever his method, the clam seems to thrive,
And this mollusk continues somehow to survive,
Though he may not be sure who's his mother.

So, Magna Cum Laude, acclaim to the clam!
Sing his praises both longer and louder!
May his progeny multiply, wax and grow fat,
As well as the rest of his kinsmen, so that
They'll be ours, on the shell, or in chowder.

William Percy Couse

EGGOMANIA

Consider the egg. It's a miracle,
 A thing so diverse for its size
That we hardly can help growing lyrical
 When given the Pullet Surprise.

The scope of this peerless comestible
 Must drive other foods to despair,
Since it's not only fully digestible
 But great for shampooing the hair;

It's boilable, poachable, fryable;
 It scrambles, it makes a sauce thicken;
It's also the only reliable
 Device for producing a chicken.

Felicia Lamport

THE COW

for Jean Pedrick

The cow's a sort of bourgeois beast:
Her peer the steer becomes a feast,
It doesn't faze her in the least;
She'd hardly pause to moo "How *triste*."

To please the latin sporting crowd
The noble bull, once snorting proud,
Is gored by sword, his great head bowed . . .
And does the cow's contentment cloud?

Of all life's horrors, here's the chief:
Her calf's made suede and baby-beef;
The cow displays no sign of grief;
She's stony as a bas-relief.

Her kin can't win? That's Nature's scheme.
At mulling cud the cow's supreme.
While others battle, mourn, blaspheme,
In narcissistic self-esteem

She stands there, giving heavy cream.

Barry Spacks

CAT SPY

He closes both eyes

and watches.

Michael Cadnum

TACKY

The limegreen gecko
likes an archipelago.
Its adhesive toes
are bulbs and bulbs
about to lose touch.
At what a slant
their bulbousness!

For an oblique,
limegreen week
the luminous Phelsuma
unglues you
with its *ge kok*!
and ceiling walk.

(What gum coheres those toes?)

Apprehensive
of prehensiles,
you sleep a humid, incoherent fit,
eyes turned upward into stare
where lizards Escher
into air
above your London coiffure.

Or your Indian Ocean
curry.

Kay Deeter

BRONTOSAURUS & CO.

There's a very simple moral to the complicated story
That concerns the giant reptiles in their momentary
      glory.
From their sudden disappearance we would argue, a
      priori,
That they felt that it was wiser to be safe than to be
      saury.

Robert N. Feinstein

MOVE OVER, URI GELLER!

He stares at the door
And his molecules buzz
And will it to open
And lo! It does!
Unblinking, he stares
At his empty dish
And presto! It's filled
With his favorite fish!
My cat has a power
At his command
To psychokinetically
Move my hand!

Dorothy Heller

THE TWO-FACED CAT

I.

Cats are dainty
Cats are clean
Cats are purry
When they dream

Cats are playful
Cats are fun
Cats lie in
The morning sun

Cats are cuddly
Cats are cute
Cats can clean
Their furry suit

Cats are kindly
Cats are sweet
Cats land always
On their feet

II.

Cats are mousey
Cats are mean
Cats scratch holes
In your new screen

Cats are sneaky
Cats are sly
Cats will look you
In the eye

Cats are lazy
Cats are fat
Cats do nasties
In your hat

Cats are pious
Cats are rude
Cats stare at you
When you're nude

Charles Ghigna

THE ELAND AND THE OXFORD

(Eland; n.—The South African antelope)

In ancient Lithuanian
The *elnis* roamed the plain;
In Dutch, the elk was *elend*,
In wind and sun and rain.

Old Slavic, *jelenis*, the hart,
In Greek, *ellos*, the deer;
In Welsh, the *elain* got its start
In an antique Celtic ear.

The Indo-European *eln*
Gave rise to French *elan*,
So eland's just a jump away—
That's how the name caught on.

Dorothy Ferster

from *SONGS OF THE SERENGETI*

Klipspringer

The klipspringer poses alone on the rock,
Away from the rest of his gang.
How did the klipspringer get to the top?
My guess is: the klipspringer sprang.

Grant's Gazelle

I've come to like the Grant's gazelle.
When it sees you come, it runs like hell.
I think its piebald rump is swell
And quite admire its horns as well.
I hear it has a lovely smell,
But was never close enough to tell.

Leopard

You may see the leopard here today.
Tomorrow you may not.
As you know the leopard's famous
For the changing of his spot.

Pyke Johnson, Jr.

OWL FEATHER TIME

IBIS CHICKEN the calendar this morning,
and I see it's my BIRDSday. Twelve SWIFT months
have flown around LARK only yesterday.
It GREBES me to see what the mirror
every MOURNING DOVEs reflect: another CROWfoot.
I used to be a COOT TOWHEEded GULL, but lately
OWL FEATHER Time has been ROBIN me
of my LARKS. I get to PUFFIN some, too,
and feel a little WARBLER.
I have to TEAL myself, Don't THRUSH so much,
GOOSE slow, don't WREN when you CRANE walk.
Time and PTARMIGAN I have wished to TERN back
the clock. Alas! C'est L'OISEAU!

But here's SWAN thing that's a HAWK of a lot
BITTERN today: I'm MOCKINGBIRDer meals
for myself—no JUNCO foods. I'VE sworn off
FLICKER. OSTRICH my BIRD brain
and I feel BITTERN mentally, No DARTER bout it.
Fact is, OWL say modestly, I feel quite
FLIGHT-eyed and BOOBY-tailed. I used to be
an introBIRD, afraid of my VIREO shadow.
What a COWBIRD I was! WATER BIRDen of EGRETS
I used to CANARY. I WOOD DUCK out of sight,
CREEPER round on tipTOWHEE, avoiding PURPLE,
FINCH away from strangers.
Now, though, I'm almost BALD, EAGLE
to SHRIKE up conversations with everyBIRDy
even with the opposite GANDER.
I keep PLOVERS too, now and then.

When I'm asked, ORIOLE friends best? I say yes,
if they're NUTHATCHER beck and call all JAY long

every SEAGULL Jay. Friendship GOOSE sour with over-
KILL, DEER and PHEASANT though the friend may be.
You can BUTCHER life I wouldn't CHUCK WILL'S
        WIDOW,
or TERN away any LOONly OWL GULL, but
        SPARROW me,
please, the company of any OWL GROUSE
SWALLOWing in self-pity, who STORKS around
RAVEN about the good LARK of others.
The VEERY worst was RUBY KING, a former
        roommate.
I never met a GALLINULE my life
as BITTERN about everyBIRDY as she was.
One day, as RUBY came INDIGO BUNTING her nose
into my affairs, I said, "TANAGER own business, RUBY,
and if FLYCATCHER reading my mail again,
OWL THRASHER tail, I will!" That was TALON her.
I said I wished she WOOD PECKER things and go.
She did.

But I don't hold GROUSES. Life is on LOON, after OWL.
We are MARTIN time HERON earth.
There's sure to be at least one good CARD-
INAL our decks. When it's our TERN, we should play it.
Nothing VULTURed, nothing gained. Soon enough
we'll have to FALCON our seat belts
for the WILD BLUE yonder. We might as well
hitch our WIGEON to a STARLING and go off
        HUMMING.

Let OSPREY it's a QUAIL of an adVULTURE!

Helen Copeland

THE JINKY JUNK

The jinky junk is a bashful bird,
It only sings when it can't be heard;
And since no watcher has heard its call
There's really some doubt if it sings at all.

Louis Hasley

NOAH'S ARK: A SAMPLING

The Bear

The polar bear provides
the eskimos their hides,
but now and then an ursa
will make it vice versa.

The Karakul

Mary had a karakul,
its fleece was black as coal,
and everywhere that Mary went
she always wore her stole.

The Lion

The lion, it is only fair,
deserves to get the lion share,
but what is left, we'd like to stress,
be given to the lioness.

The Toucan

Just as it applies to man,
two toucans, too, can live
as cheaply
as a single toucan can.

Michael Braude

I DO NOT LIKE THE BEAST

I do not like the beast, Berenice.
It is hard to be easy with bears.
But if he must live with you, please
Do not ever permit him downstairs.

Robert M. Reed

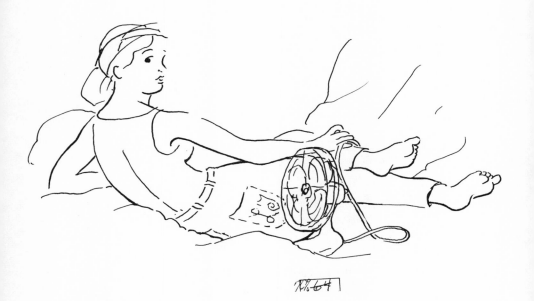

ALBA

I will arise and go now,
For I see the morning star—
But O, I do not know now
Where I parked the car.

Edward Watkins

A DIFFERENT ENDING

*Scene: The tomb of the Capulets. Juliet lies as if dead
upon her bier. Romeo, bereft, about to take poison.*

Romeo: Eyes, look your last;
       Arms, take your last embrace; and lips, O you
       The doors of breath, seal with a righteous kiss
       A dateless bargain to engrossing death!
       Come, bitter conduct! Come, unsavory guide!
       Thou desperate pilot, now at once run on
       The dashing rocks thy seasick weary bark.
       Here's to my love! (*lifts phial to drink*)
Enter Friar Lawrence, catches his arm.
Friar: Stay thy fatal intent!
       Thank God I come in the nick of time. How oft
       Tonight have my old feet stumbled at graves.
       Attend me now. A letter sent to Mantua,
       In care of Friar John, an incident of plague
       Sealed fast at its source, never to arrive.
       Had you received this missive so ill-fortuned,
       You would have found spelled plain therein a plot
       Of benefice to thee and to thy love,
       Who lies here only seeming dead, ha'ing taken,
       Faithful child, at my instructiòn,
       A potion mixed to hold her deep entranced,
       Beyond the semblance of a pulse, for two
       And forty hours, at the end of which
       Appointed spell, having eluded by
       The poignant hazard of this medicinal ruse
       That scheduled wedding with the noble Paris
       Which she detested and her family urged,
       She will, i' th' potion be exact, awake
       To be thence spirited away by you
       To Mantua and happy life thereafter.

Look, e'en now, her eyes like candles flicker,
And dawning blood ousts night's pall from her
        cheek!

Romeo (*amazed as she stirs*):
        Her body gives this tangled tale the proof.

Juliet (*sitting up*):
        Good friar. And Romeo, as guaranteed.
        Half drowned, I rise to dreams less sinister
        Than any that swam by me there below.
                                (*The lovers embrace.*)

Friar: Come, Romeo, to Mantua escape,
        And there possess your bride by night and day
        And grow habituate, as sea to moon,
        Revolving by the constant miracle
        Of Juliet's bright face, until old age
        Shall bend to earth a uniòn so rich
        In seasons reaped and little Montagues!

Juliet: As heirs shoot forth, our elders, now so wroth,
        Shall fondly vie in lavishing forgiveness.

Romeo (*looking around uneasily*):
        Well, yes, I guess this plot has saved the day;
        And yet, it doesn't leave much of a play.

                        Curtain.

                                John Updike

BOUQUET

The bouquet of the young and fair
That unbuttons blouse and breeches
Is, *inter alia*, nature's snare
To propagate the species.

                        F. C. Rosenberger

A BOX OF POPCORN

Why be shy?
Why stay at home?
Unless your appearance
is disturbing,
let's say you wear a German helmet
touring a Veterans' Home,
a box of popcorn
is all you need.

A giant box is best,
you have all afternoon.
White cardboard
with blue-red rockets flaring
is standard,
recognized at once
as a box of popcorn,
casual as a frisbee
or plaid bermudas.

Let's take the park:
munch naturally,
you have all afternoon,
lean back on a bench,
explore the paved trail
or stray through sumac and long grass,
and if perhaps you stumble on lovers,
their bodies gleaming through green brush,
smile
but if they should protest, as if you
sat on them in a dark theatre,
offer them popcorn,
save some for the ducks.

Kevin FitzPatrick

ON BEING RANK

When I was a wee smoke-peeping teen
and the greenest cowpoke
ever seen, and meanest
most cynic and obscene
daydream wooer of fair Christine,
I ruled my peers with ridicule
sported half-cocked attitudes
was boring, rude, obnoxious, cruel
over-oiled my reeking hair,
but still felt insufficient flair
to speak to fair Christine.

William Hart

BLOW

Her skirt was lofted by the gale;
When I, with gesture deft,
Essayed to stay her frisky sail
She luffed, and laughed, and left.

Paul Humphrey

WAY OUT

Daphne saw that Apollo
Was determined to follow;
So, rather than quarrel,
She turned into a laurel.

Margaret Blaker

HEIMWEH

The east wind doth blow,
And girls shall say *No*,
    And what will Dan Cupid do then,
                poor thing?

Creep in Venus's womb
To keep himself warm,
    Sulk, and butter his bowstring,
                poor thing.

G. N. Gabbard

LOVE IN THE ROUGH

On the links I met her—a dream, a looker—
She had me all in a daze;
But I was a slicer and she was a hooker
So we went our separate ways.

Louis Hasley

CARPE DIEM

There is this chick, like,
Who sits next to me in lit, like,
And I meet her at a party, like.

I make a few moves, like,
Get things warming so as to speak, like,
And wait till it is ripe, like,
To bring up carpe diem.

She puts on this very cool look, like,
Like before an exam, like,
And says she's got nothing against me, like,
Or carpeing the diem—except with me, like.

Thomas Emery

FIFI FOR LOVE

Oh do not be fooled by
the pink satin bow in her curls
the moist brown eyes shy as a girl's—

Once she buried upsidedown
her rival, Sebastian
the unwary box turtle.

Bonnie Jacobson

OLD FLAME
or, *A WOMAN OF ACTION*

When your lover invites you to join him
at dinner with his old flame
who just blew into town,

you wear your barest black dress,
unwrap black lace stockings,
slip on sandals with gold spiked heels.

You choose the jewelry which
is unmistakably real,
preferably his most recent gift.

You curl your hair, kohl your eyes,
knowing you're not as young as you used to be.
You hope she is even older.

You stock your purse
with expensive perfume,
an avant-garde shade of lipstick,

and mad money enough
to send you all home
in separate cabs.

You wonder if you should be
the first to arrive
at the medium-priced cafe,

or give them a chance
to talk. You decide
this once you will not be late.

You forget you are nursing
a fever. Perhaps
she will catch it too.

You file your nails to a point,
button your long black gloves
and sally into the dark.

Elisavietta Ritchie

THE MAJESTY OF LANGUAGE

She spoke to me in tongues,
With lips & breast & thigh,
Both wantonly & pure.
I answered her accordingly.
What did we say?
We're still not sure.

Louis Phillips

CYNIC

H. N. the. onlie. begetter.

Better perhaps smile wryly, if you smile,
In a world where guys and gals are guise and guile.

John Frederick Nims

MORE THAN YOU WANTED
TO KNOW ABOUT SEX

Small doses of rat poison (strychnine)
can stimulate the sexual interview.*
Take a pinch too much of the anodyne
and six men may walk slow with you.

Julia Older

* a fact from pop doc Reuben, M.D.

TOW JOB

His manhood rises slowly,
arches to the right.
Off balance, driven,
it's sucked into the night.

Impotent, he races after.
"Hey! Stop that! It's mine!"
A disembodied voice yells back,
"Come down and pay the fine."

He searches for his missing part
amidst the cars and trucks.
He picks it up at Harmony Street.
It costs him fifty bucks.

Barbara Goldberg

ODE ON FINITUDE

"If a man has the right to find God in his own way, he has a right to go
to the Devil in his own way, also."

—Hugh Hefner

Happy the man who likes to drive
a Porsche, drinks Grand Marnier and girls;
whose well-styled hairpiece looks alive
    with virile curls.

Whose hand is always full of aces,
whose teeth shine brightly in his mouth,
whose job in summer takes him places,
    in winter south.

Lucky as sin, who can delight
in women as they come his way,
knowing that what was here last night
    is gone today.

Who does not lose much-needed sleep
over old rules or tearful pleas,
and whose most active organs keep
    free of disease.

Thus let me live, by fortune kissed.
Thus let me die. And let no stern
religious fundamentalist
    tell where I burn.

Tom Riley

THE SINGER AND THE SONG

The singer's message: I am only a boy
And my songs and my fiddle
My only true friends.

But the woman banging her glass
On the formica bartop is receiving
Transmissions of life in the wild,

She envisions geese lifting
From a fern-bog in the peninsula
Of a state she has never visited.

Between numbers she buys him a beer
And for a moment there is no Ramada Inn:
Young man, I want to kiss you everywhere.

But he clings to character, stammers
His Thank you, but home's a distance,
And the roads up Moorhead way are slick.

To no avail. She's deaf. Changing.
Already she's a brute brown bear
In the northerly wood,

Already enjoying the scratch
She knows comes next on her rump
On the broken spruce branches.

Michael Finley

POSTLUDE

I never lust
after a man
as much as
before one

Ann Deagon

OPERATIVE REPORT

a dorsilinear incision was made over the second toe
from the metatarsal phalangeal joint

to the I.P. point distally.
the incision was deepened by sharp dissection
to expose the extensor tendon
which was transversely incised.
the head of the proximal phalanx
was delivered into the surgical wound and resected.
the dorsal proximal portion of the base
of the middle phalanx was resected.
the tendon was repaired with #000 chromic suture.
a capsulotomy was performed on the dorsal aspect
of the second metatarsal joint.
the skin was repaired with #000 silk suture
in a corrected position.
adaptic kling and ace bandages were applied.
the great toe and second toe were reinforced
into their corrective position
by the use of adhesive tape.
the patient tolerated these procedures well
and returned to the recovery room
in good condition.
the attending surgeon then drove the night nurse
to a motel where he performed a
common biological function with her.
a private detective took photographs
with a nikon camera with a telephoto lens
and an infrared filter and sold them
to the attending surgeon's wife.
the skin was repaired with #000 silk suture
in a corrected position.
adaptic kling and ace bandages were applied.
the patient tolerated these procedures well
and returned to the recovery room
in good condition.

Samuel P. Schraeger

TH'EXPENSE OF SPIRIT

Lust
is
just
mis-
er-
y,
wor-
ry
and
blame.
Brand-
name
dreck.
Ecch.

George Starbuck

PLAY IT LIKE IT LAYS

There was a young lady from Worcester
Who fell on the floor when he gorcester.
She thought, "What the Hell?"
And lay where she fell
'Til the fellow who'd gorcester sedorcester.

Lola Strong Janes

RIBALD LIMERICKS

I. After vainly invoking the Muse,
A poet cried, "Hell, what's the use!"
There's more inspiration
At Grand Central Station
I shall go there this moment and cruise.

II. A queer friend, who is peripatetic,
Writes: "Ireland, my dear, is magnetic:
The fairies and elves
Simply offer themselves—
Rather small, but most sympathetic."

W. H. Auden

MODERN LOVE

"How do I love thee? Shall I count the ways?"
Let's just get to it. That could take me days!

Bruce Bennett

ROSE

There was a young woman named Rose
Who had warts on her fingers and toes,
But the worst of it was
She was childless because
She had warts in worse places than those.

Ashley Montagu

THE MISTRESS OF MELANCHOLY

Let her head be from Prague, paps out of Austria, belly from France,
back from Brabant, hands out of England, feet from Rhine, buttocks
from Switzerland, let her have the Spanish gait, the Venetian tire,
Italian compliment and endowments.

—Burton.

I have waited so long for all the mails to come—
    one box Tuesday, another Friday parcel post—
at last I can begin. My screwdriver at *en garde,*
    my mistress first shall get a head: Those perfect
Czechoslovak eyes, Dresden blue, staring up out of

    excelsior. Like so, the China throat upon
    the Athenian shoulders, soldered without seam.
Now the paps hung, tinkling Bach, upon the Gold Coast
        chest,
    coasting neatly down to the Riviera.
The thighs from Thailand, smooth as ivory; the Mound
        of

140 •

Venus, straight from Pompeii, sloping invitingly
between Scylla and Charybdis . . . the Spanish gate.
The kneecaps imported from Hanoi, shins from
Vientiane;
those Aryan toes they floated down the Rhine!
Turn her around to get at the Queensland calves:
Clockwork

bums stupendous in their art—one's heart goes
running
down to think of the chimes we'll have! Let me get
your
back up, honey, this model from Brabant. And now these
English hands go here, these Wedgewood hands upon
the Remington arms from the good old U.S. of A.—

O Leonardo! Thou shouldst be living at this hour!
My mistress hath tire to strike the Venetians blind!

Lewis Turco

EPITAPH

Here lie the bones of Ephraim Stone,
Who left this life December 7.
His heart gave out
While bedding Molly Jones;
Death found him
Entering the gates of Heaven.

Lynda La Rocca

THE ANSWER MACHINE

I made a phone call to Susan.
The phone rang, but she was away.
And the answer machine took over
In its friendly mechanical way.
   Its brief introduction
   Gave me full instruction.
Then it waited to hear what I'd say.
   I did not hesitate
   But asked for a date
(I'd been thinking about it all day).
   I specified where
   And said we'd meet there.
And the answer machine said, "Okay."

The answer machine said, "Okay"
And repeated my message and name
In such faithful detail I was sure
That it wasn't just playing a game.
   Times change and one must
   Adapt and adjust,
Though at first I wasn't too keen
   To see my proposition
   Create a condition
That might seem a trifle obscene.
   And I hope I've made clear
   That's the reason I'm here,
Having drinks with the answer machine.

Pyke Johnson, Jr.

MENAGERIE

(poem with a first line from an anonymous fifteenth century verse)

I have a gentle cock
Its song my lady knows
It finds her in her bed astir
She murmurs as it crows

I have a shy & tiny snake
that when excited spits
My lady's fond touch draws it out
She loves to play with it

I have a pretty pussy
as black as deepest night
that bristles when I pet her wrong
& purrs when I pet her right

I have an eager beaver
toothless as a sage
It gnaws my log both day & night
& takes kisses for a wage

The cock plays with the pussy
The beaver with the snake
My lady & I laugh & sigh
until our limbs do ache

Michael Castro

THE RHYTHM BOY AND THE METER MAID

New Notes for "Lieder eines fahrenden Gesellen"

Well I'm Mel the Moth the Wanderer
   My meter maid and me
Just live in this here igloo
   With a gung-ho ukulelé

We eat harum-scarum omelets
   And maken melodye
By rubbing our legs together
   Al the nyght with open yë

I love her adagio dancing
   And the way she pronounces "pickle"
I'll tell you if I'm her tenor
   She is my vehícle

We're the arsis and the thesis too
   My meter-making sweetie and me
We read unto each other
   Lucy Maud Montgomerý

We start with a largo lead-in
   My meter maid and me
And graduate to allegro
   Ionic and trochée

Amphimacer and amphibrach
   My meter maid and me
Iambic to iambic to
   A spondaic finalé

Lepidopterodactylic
  Tetrameter are we
No *vers* is *libre* and no *mot*
  Is *juste* for *ma jolie*

MY PENIS

It likes you. I can tell
by the way it responds
to your hand. The way
it opens and closes
its little mouth
trying to speak to you
of its appreciation.
And the way it stands
straight and tall
like a gladiator
could only make me think
that it wants to impress you.
And look at the way it wags
its head with approval
when you stroke its beard—
I'm beginning to wonder
if it will ever let you go.

Jeffrey Zable

ALLISON

Allison, Allison, two meters high,
  is deliciously big but not fat;
her hair's pale enough to eat a fig by,
and blue is too dark to say of her eye,
  and she never eats soup in her hat.

Allison, Allison laughs if you say
  goodnight or good morning in Greek.
If you give her new slippers to practice ballet
and English tobacco she won't run away,
  and she might even tickle your cheek.

Allison, Allison wears a loose blouse
  and balloon-skin pants to the ball;
if she catches sight, though, of a scallywag mouse,
her voice will go up to the top of the house—
  which comes from her being so tall.

Allison, Allison, two decades old,
  has a number of sensible rules;
they include not to drink her tea if it's cold,
nor to patronize shops where chocolates are sold,
  and never to trip over stools.

Mark McCloskey

SONG WHILE ARRANGING
JASMINE AND JEWELWEED

1

You ask me, when did it begin?
When I saw you at the mercado
sniffing a cantaloupe. Ramon!
The way you held that melon it must
have ripened in your hand. That night
in the ballroom, it was your sparkling
mustache, the pearl stud in your tie.
And when you entered me it was as though
you already knew me, so sure was your beat,
so emphatic my reply. Adorado! I told you
I had many lovers. You knew I lied.

2

When you give me that cock-
eyed, cross-eyed, pie-eyed
look, oh my pet, I know
you're feeling the itch
to travel. That's when
I stick a rose in my hair,
light a cigarillo and offer
to button your spanking white
shirt. Adios, Ramon, bye bye!
I shut the door with finesse
and greet my own heart, sweet
heart, faithful dumb pumper.

3

Take care where you plant your feet,
my Latin-American strongman.
There's a hot tarantella on the tip

of my tongue. Don't tell me to shut
my mouth—I say what I please.
And if there's an earthquake I get
the doorway. So there's a dead one
floating in the milk. A cockroach here
can be rocked in a cradle. I don't
wear these pointy shoes for nothing.
I am no dumb blonde you swept away.
I play my part with proper agitation.

4

It's Sunday, and here comes Ramon.
All is forgiven, my docile lambkin!
Let's bleat together under the covers.
Come nuzzle the pale globe of my belly,
come drink from my goblet of love.

Barbara Goldberg

YOU ARE

To say this, he knelt on the earth,
his lips so close her petals moved
upon his breath, "Dear Violet,"
he said with all his heart, "you are
my most beloved flower." The next day,
with all his heart he said, "You are,"
to the rose.

Lolette Kuby

HOME-BAKED BREAD

"Nothing gives a household a greater sense of stability and common comfort than the aroma of cooling bread. Begin, if you like, with a loaf of whole wheat, which requires neither sifting nor kneading, and go on from there to more cunning triumphs."

The Joy of Cooking

What is it she is not saying?
Cunning triumphs. It rings
of insinuation. Step into my kitchen,
I have prepared a cunning triumph
for you. Spices and herbs
sealed in this porcelain jar,

a treasure of my great-aunt
who sat up past midnight
in her Massachusetts bedroom
when the moon was dark. Come,
rest your feet. I'll make
you tea with honey and slices

of warm bread spread with peach butter.
I picked the fruit this morning
still fresh with dew. The fragrance
is seductive? I hoped you would say that.
See how the heat rises
when the bread opens. Come,

we'll eat together, the small flakes
have scarcely any flavor. What cunning
triumphs we can discover in my upstairs room
where peach trees breathe their sweetness
beside the open window and
sun lies like honey on the floor.

Sally Croft

FOR NOW

"I'll write,"
she says.

"That would be nice,"
he says

not telling her
where he'll be

but noticing
she doesn't ask.

Bruce Bennett

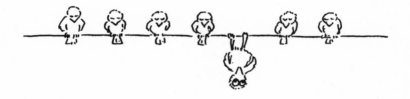

MARRIAGE

When the two become one,
I can't wait to see
which one of them
that *one* will be.

John D. Engle, Jr.

THE HITCH ITCH

"Soap under wedding ring causes skin infection."
—news headline

Though sore is the hand
With connubial band,
        Girls ask, in conjecture and wonder,
"Where is the he
To slip one on me,
        So soap can begin getting under?"

Alma Denny

TO LARRY WHO DOUBTS HE SHOULD MARRY

(from *The Psychiatrist at the Cocktail Party*)

Larry, imagine after dying that your soul
Will wake up in a barren, rural home
In India—genetically a gnome,
But smart, aware of living in a hole

From watching t.v., watching men like you
At parties, where they somberly complain
That they can't manufacture sperm like rain,
That they need "bread," though they have bread to chew.

Imagine being like you're feeling—Larry,
Who fights for Third World causes, yet who lacks
Pride in himself, who constantly attacks
America in guilty rage, won't marry

Because it's too bourgeois to make a home
With Joyce who gives you what you only give
To strangers, victims, beggars. Larry, live
As if you're not inhabiting a gnome.

Each day I hear my patients curse their fate,
How in their psyches they must re-create
Their parents tyrannizing them with guilt
Until their penises refuse to tilt,
How history seems passed on in their genes:
Oedipus zipping down his gabardines

And finding every girl feels like his mother,
Abel getting all A's despite his brother
Who beats him nightly when the lights are out
And wakes up in adulthood wracked by doubt.
I don't speak glibly when I say rejoice,
Suffer your neurosis. But marry Joyce.

Frederick Feirstein

KISSES

Kiss me, the toad said,
and take a chance
there's a curse
to be undone.

Nonsense, I said.
Besides, it's always
a frog not a toad
that gets kissed.

A frog, a toad,
what the hell! it said.

So I did and nothing
happened. I complained.

Really now,
what did you expect?
A fairy princess?
A prince perhaps?

Enough! I said.
You've made your point.

Kiss me again, it said.

I did.
It peed in my hand,
leapt off and went
bouncing through the grass.
When it reached
the clothes line pole
it suddenly became my wife
hanging the morning wash.
I ran to her
and kissed her repeatedly,
begging that she do it again
and how did she do it?

She only laughed and said
she wasn't one to kiss and tell.

You can tell me, I said.
I'm your husband for Christ's sake!

No, she said,
no no no not ever
as she bared one breast
and blew me a kiss
from behind a pillow case,
which is why I love her so.
I mean that woman knows
more tricks than a pet crow,
enough to keep me hopping mad,
not to mention hard
as a ball-peen hammer.

Roger Pfingston

THE POET'S WIFE

I may be stretched out on the bed
Composing couplets in my head:
Why is it, darling, you persist
In calling out the laundry list?

I may be sitting in a chair
Pulling rhymes out of thin air:
Why, precious, talk as you peruse
The latest items in the news?

I may be gazing out at space
Putting iambs into place:
Why stop reading a good book
To smile and say, "I *know* that look"?

Edward Watkins

LINGUA FRANKER

She hollered out, "Oh, *je t'adore!*"
   I said, "Wow! I'm delighted!"
She shouted, "I said shut the door!
   Don't get so excited!"

William Cole

LOVE'S GRAMMAR

If you were a noun
I might correct your case
to make you less possessive
or more objective.

Or if you were a verb
I might shift your voice or mood
or change your present
tense expression
to future perfect

and keep our conjugation
from suffering a declension.

Alan Nordstrom

BATTLEGROUNDS

I've fought with you in our kitchen.

I've fought with you in our bedroom.

I've fought with you in Oscar Wilde's bedroom
    at The Cadogan Hotel.

I've fought with you in a Second Empire bedroom in Paris
    looking out on those famous rooftops.

I've fought with you on the road from Paris
    while the landscape burst into Chartres.

I've fought with you on a very small island in the
    Channel I won't give away the name of,
    not even for the sake of this poem.

I've fought with you looking down from a jet
    at the Alps pushing up through the clouds.

I was still fighting with you when the plane winged down
    over Venice.

I continued that fight in a very nice bedroom there.

Had we flown on to Rome, Istanbul, or Vienna,
    I'm sure I'd have fought with you too.

There aren't many places we haven't fought.

This poem is true.

Jean Balderston

DIVORCE

One misses like a missing limb
that very special her or him;

and so one moons. One would moon less
or moon at least with more success

if that someone from whom one's parting
weren't with another someone, starting.

Robert Wallace

MRS. HOBSON'S CHOICE

What shall a woman
Do with her ego,
Faced with the choice
That it go or he go?

Alma Denny

IN THE SHOE

Oh yes, it's mine, she said, but all the rest's
With Adam, all the furniture, the horse,
That twenty year-old tart I must have shared
Him with before she even got her breasts.
But you have Alisoun, I said, and Laird,
And Tess; and you've got Max and Melanie—
But he . . . and you have Jellica, of course.
Thank God, she said. And Jude. And Barnaby.

William Wilborn

NEW SONG FOR NEW SON

This is a seagull
    and that is the sea
and this is the girl who
    unanchored me.

This is a lighthouse
    and that is the light
and this is the hiss that
    hypnotizes night.

There is a lifebuoy
    and here is your life:
oh where is the boy who
    married my wife?

Michael McFee

TRIOLET: ORAL PLEASURES

Balabusta in the kitchen
cooking meals ahead of time.
Will her husband ever catch on?
Balabusta in the kitchen,
afternoons without a stitch on,
are illicit treats a crime?
Balabusta in the kitchen,
cooking meals ahead of time.

Barbara Goldberg

DANGEROUS AGE

My friends warn,
"A man in his forties
needs watching!"

My competition
turns out to be
a generous dish

of vanilla ice cream
coupled with
the lure of the late, late show.

I'm warning friends,
"A woman in her forties
needs watching."

Donna E. Donaldson

WITH APOLOGIES TO EMILY DICKINSON

Did the harebell loose her girdle
To the lover bee?
And if she did for him, my dear,
I'll do the same for thee—
Though without my girdle, love,
I fear you'd laugh at me.
And if you know what a harebell is
Then you're one up on me.

Marla J. Sturdy

MOTHER-IN-LAW

It stops me in a sudden spot
like unsuspected chewing gum—
the sticky thought that I am what,
he fears, she will become.

Emily Otis

BIRTHDAY QUATRAIN TO A BEAUTIFUL LADY

for Astra

Grieve not the summer fled.
The snow and holly berry
Are as white and red
As cherry bloom and cherry.

F. C. Rosenberger

SILVER THREATS

You'll love me when I'm old and gray.
December love will be like May
Between us. So you say, today . . .
But I am looking far beyond
And ask, will you be just as fond
Some day when I am old—and blonde?

Alma Denny

POST MORTEM

After we two have gone, my love,
Departed like summer's rose,
Passed like the breath of dawn, my love,
Gone the way all flesh goes,

After our hands have ceased to twine,
After our song is sung,
After life's ladder—yours and mine—
Has tendered its topmost rung,

After we've traveled Yon, my love,
After life's gates have shut,
What will still linger on, my love?
Not a damn thing, that's what.

David H. Green

5

THE BEARCAT

The trouble with the Bearcat was
it ran over things,
mostly the summer
Grandfather came to live with us
after Grandma died.

Mama would get mad
about the medicine Grandfather
made in the basement
and kept in an old shed
out back of Shorty's barbershop.

Once when he took me down
to the bridge to watch the boats,
Grandfather set his medicine
in a lard can full of ice
on the front seat of the Bearcat.

The ice melted all over.
I told Mama I wet my pants.
I guess he was bad sick because
he had to take three bottles of medicine
before we got home.

That was the day the Bearcat
ran over Mama's peonies.

Maggie Greifenstein

UNCLE JOE

Let a fool throw a stone into a well,
said Uncle Joe, and ten wise men
can't get it up again. I said, Put
Carol in a bucket and *she* could get it,
and Melinda said Who would want it, anyway?
and Mother said, You're not putting Carol
into any bucket, and Uncle Jim said
Those wise men never seem to get it up.
Uncle Joe motioned for another manhattan.
One chops the wood, he said,
the others do the grunting.

Peter Meinke

VISITATION

We go in and out of Uncle Patsy's will,
and the lawyer comes back in the afternoon.
It is my will, Uncle Patsy says,
and this is my deathbed in Blasdell,
New York, and remember, he says to me,
I have given you two pink chenille
bedspreads, not one but two.

We go in and out of Uncle Patsy's will,
and the tomatoes are ripe in Steubenville,
but Uncle Patsy says these changes make all other wills
null and void, and he is taking out more insurance
on his popcorn wagon. It is my deathbed,
he says, but the doctor calls it
twenty-four hour flu.

We go in and out of the grape arbor that evening
where the men play cards, and inside, the women
wash dishes and clean Uncle Patsy's kitchen.
We are leaving in the morning, we say.
You leave me to die, he says.
You leave me for a few tomatoes and some beans.

We go in and out of Uncle Patsy's will,
and the factory smell fills the summer morning.
Come back, he cries from his bedroom.
We go into business again, get a concession
at the ball park, and this time I give you
a bigger per cent.

We go in and out of Uncle Patsy's back door,
packing the car with grapes. Come back, he says.
You're all I have. Remember the reclining chair
I gave you for Christmas. Remember the cases
of whiskey I can get wholesale.

We go back and forth, up and down the stairs,
using his bathroom, closing our suitcases.
Come back, he cries. Heartless freeloaders!
You eat my food. You take my grapes. By God,
I'll give everything I have to the nuns and priests!

We go in and out of Uncle Patsy's bedroom
while he moans and swears and demands holy water.
Goodbye, you old bastard, we say,
kissing him, wrapping him up in his bathrobe.

Julie Herrick White

MOPPING UP THE BABY'S ALTERNATIVES

"Baby, somebody down here's got it in for you."
Shel Silverstein

The baby's gotten old enough
to sit in his high chair, throwing stuff.
His duckie, his spoon, and his stuffed boar
depart his high chair for the floor.
When we reach down to pick them up
he grins and bangs his plastic cup
to thank us. Then he finds his rattle
and hurls it gaily toward Seattle.
We stoop to fetch it this once more.
He flings the rest toward Baltimore.
Jack can recognize his hand.
At five months old, he understands
that he can keep or he can throw.
He's the impresario
of choice. We've lost ours, though.
We can't have sex or French cuisine.
We can't play tennis or go skiing.
Instead I watch my little son
learning by comparison.
Will this fall faster or will that?
How fast does cereal fall? Splat.
A light goes on inside his head
but off in mine. I'll soon be dead
and my entire epitaph
will be "she couldn't pick up half
the toys and food her children dropped."
After I get this kitchen mopped
I'll adjust. I'll get on track.
I'll throw Jack (into his bed).

Jeanne Murray Walker

STUDENT AWAY

Dear daughter in that distant dorm,
I can see your sprawling form,
The scattered textbooks, notes, swirled smoke,
Candy wrappers, cans of Coke.

At home your room now rests serene,
Desk uncluttered, ash trays clean,
And, darling, though for you I pine,
This arrangement suits me fine.

Martha H. Freedman

WORKING ON A TAN

It takes work, he told me,
And you could see it did.
A tan so deep I thought at first,
Standing behind him, that his genes
Must have assisted. But no, as we shifted
Positions in the elevator, it was clear
He'd done it all himself. Incredible.
A compliment was called for, which
He accepted, like a diva, as his due.
And I wondered: *Could I, too?*

Now I'm equipped with a back yard,
Hammock, a stream with large flat
Boulders designed for basking—
All the right paraphernalia
For tanning. But I hide
Indoors with my typewriter,
Writing. The problem is
Without a lawn to mow, a patch
To sow and hoe, I am too much
A putterer to stay put.

To which the obvious solution
Has been to plant my desk out here
In the way of the sun and tan
As I finish the poem I've begun,
Its stanzas interleaved with pages
Of the ongoing novel. (I never could
Figure how anyone can justify poetry
As a full-time job. How do they get through
The day at MacDowell—filling out
Applications for the next free lunch?)

"Do I smell sour grapes?" jeers
My imaginary friend at the colony
(Whose every summer has been subsidized
For lo these many years). Her nose
Is accurate, and in this matter of a tan,
As well, it may be I am moved mainly
By envy of those whose copper tones
Betoken subsidies that need not be
Applied for—the social lions,
The skiers, the climbers, and wealth's other scions.

Who have, for all their patrimonial pelf,
Worked at their tans, while I myself
In mid-July am barely roseate.
Indeed, it is not, or it ought not be,
Their cash I covet but the care
They take to keep their carcasses
In good repair, their tans epiphenomenal
To the larger task of trimming
Sails and waists until fair Cythera,
And their abdominals, heave into view.

It can't be easy for that happy few
To leave off squeezing the wineskins
Of effortless pleasure and step into
The shoes of cowboys, farmhands,
Working stiffs. Once it was smart
To be palefaced and overfed. Now
Only hicks and mafiosi are complacently obese,
And so the bourgeoisie must work at seeming
As leisured as the class that can
Always find time for tennis and a tan.

It helps that Hollywood eroticizes
The clothing and complexions of the poor.

Without the lure of those confections
Who'd bother with cabanas at the shore?
Who'd buy the balms for quicker basting?
And what would these mosquitoes feed on,
If time and blood were not for wasting?
No doubt the race would keep on breeding,
If fashions in flesh-tones were paler,
But I'd still burn to seem a sailor.

For say what you will, a suntan speaks
Of a purpose held steady for weeks and weeks.
Even lacking the *toute ensemble*
Of a body beautiful, at least being brown
Connotes an allegiance to something primal.
When skin and sun are one on one
And the sweat that tickled starts to stream
And consciousness becomes ice cream
That melts into dreams in your hand,
Then you're in sight of the land promised the tanned.

Then the ultraviolet in the air
Reminds your melanin that *you are there*—
In Arcady beyond the reach
Of custom or of clothes, a peach
That's slowly burning into scarlet,
A fool, a simpleton, a common varlet
Asleep beside a golden veldt
Of Breughel wheat, feeling what he felt
Who first lifted his face to the sun
And said, *Turn me over, this side's done.*

Tom Disch

SUNDAY IN THE PARK WITHOUT
SOUTIEN-GORGE

I like the way a running girl bounces,
Particularly the upper ounces.

William Cole

LIMERICKS

The limerick's never averse
To expressing itself in a terse
   Economical style,
    And yet, all the while,
The limerick's *always* a verse.

A monkey sprang down from a tree
And angrily cursed Charles D.
   "I hold with the Bible,"
    He cried. "It's a libel
That man is descended from me!"

Twin sisters named Coral and Carol
Were laid out in their finest apparel.
   Their lives had been moral.
    For Carol a chorale
Was sung, and for Coral a carol.

It started with billing and cooing,
And that led me on to a wooing,
   But when we were wed
    The cooing stopped dead,
And the billing became my undoing.

The sex-life her husband dreamed of,
She considered herself far above.
   He craved osculation
   And *then* copulation!—
She wanted to kiss and make love.

In the spring I am always afraid
For the honor of young man and maid.
   I tremble with dread
   Lest a lad be misled
And I shudder to see one miss laid!

A newcomer greeted a saint:
"It's ol' Peter, goddam if it ain't!"
   "Sir, here you may use
   Any language you choose,
But, God damn it! you cannot say 'ain't!' "

"If we let the Greeks in, they'll betray us,"
Helen warned Trojan wives from her dais.
   "I fear men'll flay us,
   I fear men'll slay us,
But mostly I fear—Menelaus!"

Laurence Perrine

THE CUSTOMS OF QUEENS

A Footnote to *The Cradle of Erotica*

Wu Hu of the Great T'ang Dynasty
held court in an ornate gown
which opened up in audience
each time the men knelt down.

She stood before her retinue
and made the men go down.

Both councilor and diplomat
no matter their renown
attended her with bated breath
till after they'd gone down.
They had to keep their tongues in check
when they were going down.

This tickled her but one may reign
the other way around.
No principle applies to queens
when it comes to going down.
Queens move in a mysterious way
and have their ups and downs.

A queen may wish to use her head
and Cleopatra found
a taste for Roman visitors
with Egypt going down.
They were dying, Egypt, dying
with Egypt going down.

Ah what avails the sceptered race
when women wear the crown?
One elevates its majesty.
Another drops it down.
Wu Hu held high the royal head.
Cleopatra let it down.

Knute Skinner

THE EDDYSTONE LIGHTHOUSE*

The oddest edifice to stand
on a rocky ledge of the English strand,
a creaking polygon of wood,
imperfect pagoda built by the good
Winstanley of Littlebury,
mercer retired, who raised in a hurry
as deficient a tower as one may expect
from a whirling-dervish intellect.
He meant it as a work of art.
Its useless vanes and cranes looked smart,
so did its wooden candlesticks;
the twirling suns played dazzling tricks
with moons and cats painted in between—
the moons in blue, the cats in green—
and over the door a Latin motto,
"Glory to God, Pax in Bello."

In his temple of quirky science
Winstanley made a ghostly alliance.
If he gave his slipper a kick
a spirit would rise and menace the quick.
Win also kept a strange invention—
an old armchair of magic intention.
Quiet and cozy it sat for its master
but squeezed other parties to near disaster.
His neighbors liked Win in the main,
yet no one doubted he was insane.
He took his ale with dwarfish people,
tossed rocks on dogs from the lighthouse steeple.

* The first Eddystone lighthouse was built by Winstanley of Littlebury in
1812 and was destroyed in the Great Storm of 1816.

The morning a wreck washed ashore
Lord Mayor faced the north wind's roar
to call on Win and reason with him.
Win fished from his window and wouldn't give in
to any warning of a great storm at sea.
"Eddystone will stand for England and me."
That night when the tide engulfed the tower
Win took measurements by the hour.
The cowardly ghost left with a scream
while Win made toast and had a dream
of an ocean grotto filled with fish
well trained to serve his slightest wish.

Win and his visions were swept away.
His just reward, stuffed-shirts would say.
Those wiser praised his quaint exit
as the eddy—not the ebb—of wit.

Mary J. McArthur

IN BRUSSELS

In Brussels everyone makes lace;
   it's done quite hoi-polloi-ly.
They tat and chat and often say,
   "Another day, another doily."

Robert Wallace

LENINGRAD NOW: THE NEW DECADENCE

> "Wild-wild Western Things a Hit in the USSR
> —Blue-dzhinsy and Country Western"
> —*Christian Science Monitor* (4/13/84)

From his cab or from his dacha
in his suit or in his parka
to these hootenanovich bashes
many a droshke driver dashes.
At this borsch bar & stolyoveyar
many a muzhik from his mir
lends these waitresses an ear.
One-eared goatherds from the steppes
Volga boatmen risking reps
join the gentlemen from Schweppes.
Commissars from tallest Caucasus
come to hear what all the ruckus is.
Single and collective farmers
dig these earthy ochi charnyas.
Wearing jeans and balaclava
sampling caviar & halávah
sipping samovar's espreetski
(not that vodka's off lim-eetski)
patrons rave, the show is socko;
watch those waggish steppers walk, oh!
Even the portly Astrakhan
throws portfolio in ashcan;
balalaikas best inform him,
Country Western dawns upon him!
("Hey, tovarich! You, Sir Comrade
in the dzhinsy! Backsheesh, please!
Do come back and don't be sheepish!")

A. L. Lazarus

PLACE NAMES

I.

If there's a lack
of Happy Jack
with only two,*
these happy few!

II.

Nebraska has Ong;
New Jersey, Ong's Hat;
when both belong
much closer than that.

III.

When two in Bush, Kentucky,
take wing and fly away,
the hunter will, if lucky,
find Bird in Hand, Pa.

Ernest Kroll

* In Arizona, Louisiana.

PROPER BOSTONIANS

Proper Bostonians do not discuss
On subway train or crowded bus
The late Professor Irving Babbitt's
Personal habits.

They will not, waiting in a line
At a shopping center in Brookline,
Lead one to think all does not go well
With any Lowell.

They never, in a public hall,
Mention a Cabot or a Saltonstall,
Or refer, though Time and Boston pardon her,
To Mrs. Jack Gardner.

Proper Bostonians, when together,
Speak guardedly of Boston's weather;
Other subjects they are prone
To leave alone.

William Jay Smith

SAVANNAH LADIES

for Mimi

Two old ladies, friends since girls,
In a neighborhood going down, visited
In the late afternoons when it grew cool
Enough to walk the few blocks between their houses,
Small, tidy houses where a pan or kettle
Could be heard in any other room, all
Of the rooms rather packed like a leather trunk
With lamps, vases, mantel pictures, cushions,
Houses as crowded as their small mossy yards
Where flowers, shrubs, and broken fruit trees
Grew to the sagging sidewalk gate. They
Visited until after dark when they were together,
The walk a little longer every spring as the days
Grew longer, which was the best visiting time,
Bringing music and laughter out of doors all 'round,
Until one spring evening late, one old friend in
Her goodbyes to the other, said, You
Would be so kind to walk me home.
And the other complied. Then arrived
At the second house they visited longer
Until it was the visitor's time to leave
And she said, It's got so late now, I
Can't see how I can make that walk alone.
And her hostess, winding herself in a wrap,
Agreed to walk the few blocks, since her
Friend had done the same for her. And there,
The first to make the walk in the afternoon,
Hating to leave this talk and lamplight and
Go back in the dark, expressed her fear,
Which her friend understood, although
This time she had to decline, hardly
Having the legs left to rise for goodbyes.

So they did what they always did with
Troubles of this nature, on their knees
On a throw rug under the mantelpiece.
They asked for an answer and waited
In the dim light inside, sirens and
Cars flashing by in the flashy street,
Until a voice in the hush between cars
Out in the city night said, Taxi!
But the visitor with her house so far
Had not anything with her to pay a fare.
But we have had an answer, said her friend,
We will have another. Call, she said,
Which they did and told the driver their trouble
When he came, explaining their long afternoon
And their walks and their situation, which
He understood. So they were glad again,
Waved and said goodbyes again. Goodbye,
Said the lady through the taxi window.
Next week, said her friend at the cracked gate,
And don't forget your taxi money.

Wallace Whatley

BONELESS ON THE MONON

Riders on the Monon in December,
let's forfeit all our bones!
Let snowy fields glide by
and breakable glass ponds;
the skaters in molasses plaids,
courtesy of Currier & Ives.
Depend upon this team of diesels
to neigh along the rails,
their tow-chains clanking,
their sledges swaying.
Chuck the sleighs—they've got us saddled!
Their manes are flying in our faces!
On, Percheron! On, Charger!
Now we gallop past the silos,
corn cribs, hogs magnificent in mufti;
past the stilted tanks, the formal water
blessing out the towns
of Battle Ground and Chalmers,
Rensselaer and Hammond.
We must hoot at V-8 horses stalled at crossings,
buried in snow sidings.
Near the Windy City
if winds whip up harsh names
they cannot harm our bones:
by the Monon's horses hypnotized
equestrians pull boneless
into Dearborn and Van Buren.

A. L. Lazarus

TABLE FOR ONE

I am a sucker for ambience.
Like the intimate French restaurant
downstairs, dim, with posters of Nice,
but "table for one" is awkward to say.
The waiter, proud of his massive menu,
led me to a niche in the corner
as if I were improperly dressed.

Then the whole bit—mussels meunière,
Dover sole with Montrachet in bucket,
chocolate mousse, coffee, and brie.
A petty hedonist out on a spree.

Mostly tables of double couples
smiling in starch and fur.
Time to muse, to stare
at honey-crusted bread, time
to play a role or wiggle toes.

Now, I am no fool for happiness.
I noted the lout who snapped at his love
till she left, looped, for the john
while he ogled the sultry one by the door,
but dining out alone is a bore.

Francis J. Smith

SEA GRIEVER

I must go down to the seas again
  before the beach becomes
A mass of reddened bodies
  backed by condominiums,
And all I ask is a tiny slit
  in a beach umbrella's dome
Through which to glimpse the breakers
  with their crests of styrofoam.

I must go down to the seas again
  through the popsickle sticks and foil
And salty spray that's tainted
  by the scent of suntan oil,
And all I ask is a rivulet
  twixt the offal streams from boats
And the slick spills from the offshore drills
  where the hapless seagull floats.

I must go down to the seas if but
  to see Poseidon scowl
At water so polluted that
  his fish are crying "Foul!"
While he weeps at desecration
  too abhorrent to be faced:
His wine-dark sea a potpourri
  of radioactive waste.

Felicia Lamport

STAYING POWER

I always unravel
Whenever I travel,
And so I stay home with the few,
Serene and immobile,
Whom those who go global
Can send all their bright postcards TO!

Maureen Cannon

TRAVELING COMPANIONS

Hard-drinking Aunt Maude from Montana
Took her sister to visit Havana.
Maude went, she told some,
For fresh fish and good rum.
"And I needed cigars," said Aunt Hannah.

Lynda La Rocca

SONG OF THE OPEN ROAD

The Interstate goes mainly straight.
Sometimes around. Or up. Or down.

Woods pass by. Some barns and houses.
Fields with tractors, fields with cowses.

Robert Wallace

● 185

COCK-A-DOODLE-DON'T

At this old inn that caters to lovers,
shutters prolong the amorous nights.
Dawn goes unheralded day after day;
the rooster is wooden at *Le Coq Muet*.

Anne Marple

THE SANDHILLS OF NEBRASKA

You will be on vacation,
driving your wife, your three kids,
and your yapping poodle
across the Sandhills to South Dakota

to see Mount Rushmore.
Twenty-five miles from the nearest town
you will see the first windmill
off in the distance on a hill.

Why would anyone drill on a hill?
you wonder, but decide it doesn't matter:
the windmill's tail is loose,
the wheel goes on spinning hellbent for election.

And your kids have been counting.
Fifty-six thousand fence posts,
two crows eating a dead rabbit, one snake.
And you think, *The only steer*

I've seen since Burwell is that
white-faced angus by that windmill,
thirsty, no doubt,
and skinny as a rail.

And you notice there's not much grass out here,
just a lot of sand and blowouts.
Blowouts worry you.
You simultaneously hope your car doesn't get one,

and that you have enough air in your spare.
You say aloud,
We'd be up shit-creek without a paddle then.
(Your wife says, *What, dear?*)

And you are, because two miles later
the right front blows leaving you stuck
right smack dab in the middle
of the biggest damned sandbox

your kids have ever seen.
You're wondering how Lawrence of Arabia
would handle this. You're sixty-nine thousand,
four hundred forty fence posts,

three crows, and two dead rabbits
from the nearest town. You look at your spare.
It's as flat as a sheep-herder's daughter.
So everyone piles out of the car,

including that stupid poodle.
And it's hot.
Your wife fans herself with a Black Hills
tourist map, your kids kick dust.

And as the poodle lifts its leg to piss steam,
you can only hope he'll evaporate.
Instead, he's busy barking at sunflowers.
You imagine a bee the size of a bull

mistaking him for a daisy and sucking him dry,
that you bury him in a badger hole,
thinking, *It serves him right*,
while your wife, dabbing her eyes with a kleenex,

tells you to say a few words
(*For the kids' sake*). Right now,
they're off chasing magpies,
your wife is looking for shade.

You wish you had a cold beer.
You wish your wife and kids
would dry up and blow away.
But when a hungry gopher gives you the eye,

you wish you could blow away, too, -
believing at the same time,
With my kind of luck I'd get stuck to a fence.
And you're wondering just how long

you're going to be stuck *here*.
Your wife has her shoes off
and is picking her toenails.
Your kids have a turtle turned upside down.

And when you're about to walk
to the nearest ranch house,
some five thousand fence posts away,
a cowboy shows up, driving a Scout.

He's wearing a plaid shirt with shiny buttons,
Tony Lama boots made from artificial alligator hide,
a beat-up white Stetson,
and a pair of stiff Levis.

His belt, hand-made in Taiwan,
has the name *Tex* engraved on it.
You think, *He must be from Texas.*
What you don't know is that he's from Maryland.

That doesn't matter. What matters
is he's going to help you.
That's the Code of the West.
He hitches you up and pulls you

to the nearest Champlin station,
the Great Name in the Great Plains.
He doesn't ask you what happened,
doesn't care where you've been.

After all, he's done this maybe
eighty-seven thousand times before,
fought off more hungry gophers
than you can shake a stick at,

put wells on top of hills.
As they say out here,
straight as the crow flies,
Nothing surprises him.

Mark Sanders

KENT SAYS

Kent says it doesn't matter
if the captain has a heart attack
or nips back for a piss. A
computer flies the plane.

Kent says that he snorts coke
before he takes his DC9 from
Dallas to Detroit. It doesn't
matter what the weather does. A
computer flies the plane.

Kent says United cabin crew
screw best. Delta's come
in second. Sank a fifth of
Jack Daniels one time,
trans-Atlantic, watching 'Superman'
in coach class. What of it? A
computer flies the plane.

If the computer fails
the back-up takes control:
if the back-up fails,
a second in-flight back-up
does the job. A
computer flies the plane.

And if that fails, Kent says,
he has to zip his pants,
blow his nose, pat the hostess
on her ass, drain his glass
and fly the goddam jet.

If Kent fails, he says,
we're in the shit.

Martin Booth

FLIGHT ATTENDANT

"What mad pursuit?"—Keats

Under her wing we men adjust to heights,
lusting after skies like troglodytes.
Disaster is the last of several odds
and ends we think about; her gods, our gods
(among them the bold pilot who inspired
her poise?). Oh subtly scented, clipped, attired
for feeding various hungers at the cart,
she keeps male travelers and ennui apart.
Did ever Fates contrive by storm or fire
or fuses blown or engines split to wire
such fantasies to pass the tedious miles
as trail her tailing down the endless aisles!
While she performs her Grecian Urn-like feats,
what ravishments, or none, strap us to seats?

A. L. Lazarus

EAT FRUIT

Keep your legs crossed, my mother said. Drinking
leads to babies. Don't hang around street corners.
I rushed to gulp moonshine on corners, hip outthrust.
So why in the butter of my brain does one marble tablet
shine bearing my mother's commandment, eat fruit?

Here I stand, the only poet from whom
you can confidently obtain after a reading
enough mushy battered brownish bananas to bake bread
should you happen to feel the urge at ten
some night in East Lansing or Boise.

You understand how needful it is, you say,
that I should carry the products of Cape
Cod such as oranges and kiwis with me
because surely they sell none in Seattle.
Suppose South America should be blockaded?

Others litter ash, beer cans. I leak pits.
As we descend into Halifax while my seat partner
is snorting the last of his coke, I am the one
choking as I gobble three apples in five minutes,
agricultural contraband always seized at borders.

Customs agents throw open my suitcase and draw
out with gingerly leer from under my negligee
a melon. Drug smugglers feed their self importance,
but me they hate along with the guy trying to smuggle
in a salami from the old country his uncle gave him.

I am the slob who makes gory stains on railroad seats
with fermenting strawberries. You can recognize me

by the happy cloud of winged creatures following my
        head.
I have raised more fruitflies than genetics labs.
I have endowed ant orphanages and retirement
        communities.

However, I tell you smugly, I am regular in Nome,
in Paducah, in both Portlands and all Springfields.
While you are eating McMuffins I am savoring a bruised
but extremely sophisticated pear that has seen five
airports and four cities and grown old in wisdom.

Marge Piercy

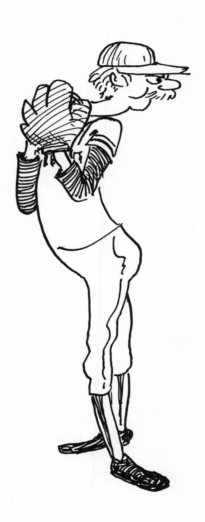

6

THE FALLEN THUMBTACK

You hunt it high,
  You hunt it low.
Does the naked eye
  Espy it? No.
It's spotted by
  The naked toe!

Alma Denny

UNNECESSARY

Needless to say,
it's needless to say
what it's needless to say.

That is to say,
it's not necessary to say
what it's needless to say.

There! I've hit the nail right on the head:
what it's needless to say needn't be said.

James Steel Smith

ENTERTAINING POSSIBILITIES

This must be observed
sedulously. Possibilities
are particularly sensitive
to drafts and omissions
and given to a delicacy of
digestion. When possibilities
are entertained along with facts,
it must be the possibilities who
are first offered the snacks
and drinks. It is not important
what a fact thinks.

Kay Ryan

GIVE ME AN A

Give me an A
A capital
as Dürer made A and D his own

A calls the other letters
in all the languages
come here   come here
Q peculiar   necessary U
roll me over R and steadfast I
says A

and cheered or grumbling
bumping up against each other
getting out of line becoming words
and lining up they're characters

Caroline Knox

Sincere Apologies

Dear Sir: This is in reply
    To your inquiry of the sixth.
We can't give you the info till
    We get this darn thing fixed.

Alma Denny

OUTSTANDING EXCEPTION

To show my resolve
I always stand firm,
And I like to stand tall
While others squirm.
When the chips are down
I often stand pat,
And I'll surely stand by
If it comes to that.
I'll even stand down
(And I might resign),
But I never stand out
When I stand in line!

Ned Pastor

WRONG TURNINGS

Hoist by his petard:
A lawyer disbarred.

An actor displayed;
A fighter defrayed.

A rancher deranged;
Bank teller unchanged.

A spinster dismissed
(When properly kissed).

Robert N. Feinstein

FULL PROFESSORS

The full professors I know got
full by gradual degrees.
Still it's interesting to note
their varying capacities.

Jim Wayne Miller

THE PROFESSOR'S MAIL

Stuffed in my office box each day by four,
fliers, memos, processed letters addressed
"Dear Colleague"—trash to clutter a cluttered
afternoon, settling on my life like the day's
repast of dirt (we eat a bushel, they say,
before we're through). A quick glance, mutter,
and pitch the lot. While still alive or less
than a few years cold, I'm in for more:
a small woods, at least a full-grown tree,
pulped for every anyone, including me.

But, what's this! just beneath the notice
of the Lost Committee meeting, now reset
for yesterday in Flying Dutchman Hall
—a certified letter, addressed by hand, which grants
me understanding, plus a small estate in France.
Or so I thought and, disregarding all
the signs, will keep on thinking till I get
the yellow slip that says, "Your dean informs us
of excessive absences and grade sheets overdue
since your death last year, and so we're docking you."

William Trowbridge

THE HISTORY OF THE WORLD

Ectoplasm in the air! A partial eclipse
of the moustache and a nineteenth century
German idealist climbs a fever, giving birth
to the phenomenology of the nose

that understands what's written on the wind
of the right nostril is engraved in the ring
around the left . . . In San Francisco
strange handkerchiefs travel under the counter

at the speed of light. A nose at birth begins to die
and the end begins at the beginning. The imperfect
shadow of a stuffed nose is the new poetic.
Believing the soul resides in the nose, a fourteenth

century wife of a Castillian aristocrat, having learned
her husband was going to guillotine her nose
as a wedding present for her successor, stuffed it
with holy water, myrrh, and a wad of honeycomb.
         Wilhelm

Reich stuffed his with a mixture of fermented sharks
              meat
and illuminated scrolls that describe St. Joseph
riding a tortoise around a recumbent Virgin
submerged in a goblet of steam glazing her Wedgewood

nostrils. A nun, lowering the drawbridge
for a priest, wore a black handkerchief over her face
for thirty years that lifted in the wind
of her devotions. You can't xerox a stuffed nose

leaping from a Lady Godiva
chocolate covered peach to a bowl of gelatinous
red and yellow antihistamines. Raiders of a nose shaped
pyramid of the Upper Nile opened a delicatessen

on the Lower East Side. In Los Angeles, unemployed
dairy farmers injected silicone into the clear passages
of go-go dancers until both nostrils filled to Renaissance
proportions. As the gold trumpet of the herald

bloomed in the stratosphere, the imperfect
shadow of a horn of plenty was set in heaven
and sat on a throne. Doc Holiday and Wyatt Earp
filled theirs with lead balls, black powder,

and spun the chambers. If the eye
of the nose intercedes for the rectum,
can the state of repose achieved by Erasmus,
fallen from his mount with kidney stones in 1506,

be far behind? In Palm Beach, a full nostril's
looked upon as a sign of breeding. Speaking
from the nose is regarded as more etheric,
godlike . . . Another poet, believing his nose

was haunted by W. H. Auden and Jesus Christ,
relied on an Ouija board to speak for the spirits.
Black market transistorized nose hair cutters
laundered off the coast of Florida are highly prized

by libertines and vegetarians tumbling
out of one nose into another. Queen Victoria
negotiated a liquor license for the Prince of Wales'
nose, the swinging doors of his nostrils opening

into the twentieth century, where Frank
Lloyd Wright was waiting to model the first skyscraper
after a cue tip. An old man with three nostrils
and a bad cold is looked upon with no little reverence

in the back rooms of the Kremlin. How sweet the aroma
rising from the appetite of one who wished
Weingarten's nose was filled with nickels. Whither
the years and who can remember. O sinusitis, mingling

with love and poetry, lead the way through ivy covered
stations of the cross into inner sanctum of the ear drum,
where I may live out my life, holding up the cocoon
of my nose to the inner light, like a glass paperweight

to a window, watching the wings of my godlike self, my
          hermit
almost ready to fly. My stuffed nose I do bequeath
to our great brother Villon and to the earth our mother
I bequeath a tincture of goldenseal and the common cold.

Nicolai Vasilievich Gogol dropkicked a nose
baked in a piroshk and wearing a uniform
down Nevsky Prospect, swearing under his breath
that a stuffed nose can live twenty-seven thousand

days without a hankie, but a clean handkerchief
will die of heartbreak in a dark pocket. Amen.

Roger Weingarten

HOW DO YOU SAY "MEATHEAD" IN NORWEGIAN?

Bonanza's showing in Japan,
Get Smart is big in Britain,
And in the wilds of Yucatan
Mary Hartman has them smitten.

Gilligan, Gunsmoke, Hawaiian Eye
Are seen in lands assorted;
Old TV series never die—
They only get deported.

Keith Casto

POINTS OF VIEW

Artist: I am in love with blue.
          I squiggle it over my heart.
          Blue are my butterfly nets
          And the butterblue flies of my art.

          Painting my canvas red,
          Lolloping streaks of green,
          Blue is the color I squirt
          On the canvas I've never seen.

Critic: Influenced less by Degas,
          And a little bit less by Klein,
          This artist dotes on red;
          His is a red valentine.

Artist: I drift through oceans and skies.
          I eat ageratum stew.
          I shall exchange my brown, brown eyes
          for eyes of forget-me-not blue.

Patron: His is a flaming soul:
          Observe his red design.
          I see him influenced least by Degas—
          And a little bit least by Klein.

John Unterecker

ON "THE SLEEPING GYPSY" BY HENRI ROUSSEAU

A gypsy
has fallen
into sleep
next to her
6-string lute
& carafe.

The moon is
full & round;
a few stars
speckle blue.
Hills in the
distance look
like   hills.

Some lion
keeps walking
into &
out of the scene,
half-hoping
to get in
the picture.

David Brion McCoy

THEY BARELY MADE IT

In much of recent cinema
Clothing is at a minema.

Keith Casto

EINE KLEINE LIGHT MUSIC

A Sequence

i

Like most other intelligent folk
wise Ludwig thought money no joke!
He was sure that no gold
was in the music of old
and so died without going Baroque.

ii

Composers live slow and live fast—
most have a good time while they last:
it's known to us all
Joe Green had a *Ball*
and Smetana—he had a *Vlast*!

iii

Some men sell their souls for a lady,
some ladies go ape over Haiti;
Satie had a case
on an ancient Greek vase
and called his disease *gymnopédie*.

iv

If you're one of those people who pooh-pooh
the excesses of Alban Berg's *Lulu*,
recall that Rameau
was often *de trop*
and Tchaikovsky was usually tutu.

v

Once Ferde—who hated progressions—
was missing from one of his sessions;
he was found in the heat
composing a suite
in a state of the deepest depressions.

E. R. Cole

THE JADE BOX AND THE CRITIC

The intricately carved green grapes and foxes
In polished jade, the lapidary skill,
The ancient art, the elegance, all will
Count little if he does not care for boxes.

F. C. Rosenberger

POST-STRUCTURALIST CRITICISM

Too many leaps,
doesn't sit still like it should.
Keeps floating
clear off the page.

Spindly
where it should be strong.
Thin and blue, breast milk
when we wanted cows.

A dozen or so, mooing
in the field.
Black and white, fat heifers
on green grass.

Make the grass tall fescue.
Wait until fall before planting.
For God's sake fence it off
till it starts growing.

Judith Skillman

A CANDID ASSESSMENT

W. Aloysius Merrick
admits his poems are esoteric;
says, "One doesn't write them for
the folk in Chattanooga,"
says, "One must candidly assess
what one does as 'caviar
to the general.' "
                    Well, yes—
but not the best beluga.

Vonna Adrian

THE CRITIC ON A TWO-LINE POEM

very nice but
for the dull stretches

Kenneth Funsten

WICKED AGATHA MANEUVERS US DOWN THE GARDEN PATH YET AGAIN

The Master has altered his will—
At high noon he drops dead with a cry!
Who in this household would kill?
      Did the Butler do it?
      If he did, he'll rue it—
For he has no alibi.

The Wife was at the Doctor's. She said.
Ask her Lover if this is true.
She was awf'lly shocked her husband was dead.
      Did the Butler do it?
      How do you construe it?
Wife? Doctor? Lover?—Who?

There's a Sister who's a heller—
A rotten Nephew—gets in fights—
A crazy Aunt lives in the cellar—
      Did the Butler do it?
      Or did Grandma beat him to it?
All had motives—parasites.

How about the live-in Teacher?
Or that angelic Brat—
A quite precocious creature?
      Surely the Butler did it—
      Then took the knife and hid it—
No kid's as diabolical as that.

While we are searching for a clue—
All the tricks are in the book—
There happens Murder Number Two.
      The Butler didn't do it.

If he did he blew it.
For he's the Corpse . . . The Cook?

He clapped the tea-cakes in to bake—
Then scurried up the stairs—
    For God's sake—?

                              Mildred Nelson

WHERE HE STANDS ON SEX AND POETRY

i was talking to my buddy
on the phone
and he said
wait a minute
my girlfriend's taking
my pants off
can you call me back?
and i said
i thought you
wanted to talk about poetry
and he said later.

                              Samuel P. Schraeger

CRITIC

A teacher in Kalamazoo
Was asked if she fancied *haiku*.
Said she, "They've got class,
You bet your sweet ass,
But aren't they a mite cutesy-poo?"

David H. Green

A LESSON OF THE MASTER

The good girl has no story—so
Guy de Maupassant teaches:
We cannot look on virtue bare,
But only in her breaches.

Leonard Trawick

THE PORNOGRAPHER EXPLAINS HIS ART

The words come
by themselves.

Bruce Bennett

LOST LEAVES FROM THE GREEK ANTHOLOGY

It was like Doric honey yesterday
telling them to their faces
what I thought of them.

Today they are improved.

Now they are too good to see me.

*

Antiphanes caught and skewered
a thousand skittish lambs
while his sword saw active duty.

Now that he's hung it over the mantel
they nuzzle his hand in the street.

*

On the Areopagus
men can believe anything.

Very few do.

*

Dion, to live long,
shunned wine,
drank only water.

Here he lies
having drunk his fill
then washed up on the beach.

*

Antipater keeps a bunch of roses by him .
while he figures how to gyp people.

He smells his own scheming the less.

*

Drusilla is a democrat;
she thinks all men are equal.

All's well until you smell the rat
that scurries in the sequel:

All men come short by just two letters;
all women, therefore, are their betters.

*

Cleomenes the misanthrope
buys another new robe today
thinking it will make others admire him.

It catches spittle as well as the last.

*

When Philodemus taught,
his students were attentive as jackals.

Then when he was drained they taunted and carped.

Now they have their own students
attentive as jackals.

*

Erinna is demanding.
Bored with searching
for larger and larger men and
trying to convince them she's a virgin,
she buys an ass.

An elegant solution.

*

Some who glimpse these
will think that I, Ancrises,
lived them all. Not true.

At supper, instead
of complimenting the cook,
they want an account of how
the onion plants were fertilized.

*

Cleon judges everything
by its tastiness:
this country is boring,
that whore is refreshingly different.

All that's needed to teach him a lesson
is some delicious poison.

*

Memnon, it seems, has heard
a legend of buried treasure.

Some oracle has told him
it lies between a woman's legs
but didn't say which one.

*

Mellipus has ordered his slaves
to stop reading poetry to guests at supper.
They listen now to chatter from Mellipus.

An economical host.
What with indigestion
they eat less.

John J. Brugaletta

MILTON'S SIXTH LATIN ELEGY, CONDENSED

I'm hungry, friend, and I can't write
a serious poem, though I do dig your style.
Your letter (I got it) said how every night
the ladies made not writing worth your while.

To write the good stuff, not the usual junk
we're sick of reading in the magazines,
man, you got to get yourself good and drunk
and make the most of mythological scenes.

You know those Greeks and Romans fooled around
with jazz millenia past—not New Orleans
but stuff you could dance to, naked, real sound
too good to waste on girls in shackled jeans.

No hepper cats than Waller, Monk or Blake,
those gods and seers had their way with words,
and some of the best pickers, then, were Greek,
like Orpheus and Homer—at least two-thirds.

I tell you, man, you got to really sing
to make those groovers boogie in their graves.
Even Jesus wanted us to bring
a little rock 'n' roll to free the slaves.

David Mason

A 3rd STANZA FOR DR. JOHNSON & DONALD HALL*

I put my hat upon my head
And walk'd into the Strand,
And there I met another man
Who's hat was in his hand.

The only trouble with the man
Whom I had met was that,
As he walked swinging both his arms,
His head was in his hat.

Of course the head within the hat
Belonged to my friend Otis,
But I, since I am quite polite,
Pretended not to notice.

Louis Phillips

* 1st stanza by Samuel Johnson
2nd stanza by Donald Hall

A MOMENT IN DOVE COTTAGE

"Oh, the darling! Here is one of his bitten apples."
Dorothy Wordsworth's *Grasmere Journal*

Nowhere else in all of Britain
Was sister so with brother smitten.
With due regard to whose dental
Imprint the apple bore, her gentle
Cooing seems excessive. Fitter
To toss the object out with litter
And utter with housewifely vim,
"*Ugh*! How untidy of him!"

Vonna Adrian

BALBOA REPLIES TO JOHN KEATS

Your kind of travel is the easy kind.
You open up a book, and there you are,
around your western islands—not too far
away to shut the book, turn off your mind,
and sleep at home that night. The realms you find
are gold unguarded, goodly through and through.
The trouble in them never touches you.
Your worst discomfort is a sore behind
from too much sitting still. Yours truly, though,
paid for his travels, suffered, finally died
beheaded, that that ocean might be his
and Spain's. But does your sonnet say so? No.
You—English, ignorant, self-satisfied—
give every shred of credit to Cortez.

Tom Riley

HARDLY HARDY

I propped my arm up in a crotch
    Sloppy from the drizzle
And solemn as an oak, swore off the scotch
    And tossed aside my swizzle.

The countryside began to sway—
    It slobbered residues,
While sinking to its knees as though to pray
    The sun heaved up its hues.

Then from above I thought I heard
    A small trill voice which said:
Beware; beware; beware! The falling *bleep*.
    And something hit my head.

Well I'll be damned, it was a bird
    That spoke to me that time;
Yet marvellous the more, it had been censored
    By the Great Face behind.

Burt Beckmann

IF A.E. HOUSMAN HAD TRIED TO HIT
BIG LEAGUE PITCHING

When I was one-and-twenty
    I heard a wise coach say,
"Swing hard, and do it daily—
    A thousand swings a day;
And hit behind the runner
    'Til it comes naturally."
But I was one-and-twenty,
    No use to talk to me.

When I was one-and-twenty
    I heard him tell me this,
"You try to pull all pitches,
    And that is why you miss."
Advice? He gave me plenty;
    I ignored his fine critique.
Now I am two-and-twenty,
    And got released last week.

Gene Fehler

IF RICHARD LOVELACE BECAME A FREE AGENT

Tell me not, fans, I am unkind
    For saying my good-bye
And leaving your kind cheers behind
    While I to new fans fly.

Now, I will leave without a trace
    And choose a rival's field;

For I have viewed the market place
And seen what it can yield.

Though my disloyalty is such
That all you fans abhor,
It's not that I don't love you much:
I just love money more.

Gene Fehler

IF ROBERT FROST MANAGED THE YANKEES

Whose bat this is I think I know.
It's caked with pine tar high and low.
The Goose is shivering with fear
To think how far the ball might go.

I'll wait until defeat is near
And then I'll suddenly appear
To make those foolish umpires take
Away the win K.C. earned here.

So what if George Brett's heart will break?
The pennant race is still at stake.
And though my tactic might seem cheap,
I'm out to win, make no mistake.

The pine tar's lovely, dark and deep
Enough to make the Royals weep.
This victory is ours to keep,
This victory is ours to keep.

Gene Fehler

SMALLER ELEPHANTS, COOLER POEMS

In the land of Kalevala
off the bluffs of Beowulf
they use pairs of tusks for tog-hooks
on the backs of bath-house doors.
So that as one broods on birth-bench
the rest of the elephant
like a ton of recollection
may crash at any second
through fragile stall and time-frame.
It is then, in such a tension—
the steam ascending, the trumpeting
not too well tempered—
one may sweat the inspiration
of pygmy pachyderms
tiny and new as Marianne Moore's real toads
and infinitely more negotiable
than saunas full of ivory, saunas full of gold.

A. L. Lazarus

NEW HAVEN

John Hollander,
steering his colander,
came at last to the lands where the Jumblies live.
"Oh look," the Jumblies said, "it's Western Civ!"

George Starbuck

THE LITTLE NUISANCES

1. Nature In The Raw

The squeak of a hostess
as she sees, over your shoulder,
a more important guest arriving . . .

The squeak of the caterpillar
of the Death's Head Hawk Moth . . .

2. Haiku: Great Composers

Monteverdi. By
Rodgers and Hart? Surely just
"Mountain Greenery"?

3. Haiku: A Japanese Dried Flower At A Poetry Reading

Take a poet. Drop
him in alcohol. He'll ex-
pand in full colour!

4. T. S. Eliot and Ezra Pound

Eliot loved the music halls
(and he probably loved pantos).
Pound took the rubbish out of *The Waste Land*
and put it all into the *Cantos*.

5. Not Peace But A Sword

Mosque or temple, church or steeple,
religions are keenest
on killing people!

6. *Haiku: G.M.Hopkins*

> "I got a sudden revelation when I looked at the facsimile poem in Desmond Flower's *English Poetic Autographs*: I exclaimed, aghast at the hand writing, "That man bites his nails'. 'Yes,' said Grete (our tame-but-wild graphologist) 'and has other comfort habits!' "
>
> —Robert Graves, letter to James and Mary Reeves

G. M. Hopkins? Could
it be Genital Massage?
It seems quite likely!

7. *Ruperta Bear's Feminist Poem*

We live in a society that's phallocratic
but we're beginning to make literature cunnicentric.
Already many women can only read books by women—
if they accidentally read something written by a MAN
at once a horrible feeling comes over them,
the words grip them like the hands of a rapist,
with a scream they throw the book from them!

8. *69*

Today is my birthday, I'm
soixante-neuf!
I'm not a *cochon*
or a *boeuf*!
And, thank the Lord, I'm
not a *veuf*!
What's more, I still possess
les oeufs!

Gavin Ewart

POET LEAPS TO DEATH

Here's double grief now. Honest John, I'm numb
Not at your loss alone—good verse struck dumb.
But—lord!—for that flux of elegies to come!

John Frederick Nims

PHYSIOLOGY

"A Whitman-type, that's me! Vast! Free! Profuse!"
    I know some things are more a nuisance, loose.
"But you!—all knotted, trim, taut, rigid—ugh!"
    I know some things are better that fit snug.

John Frederick Nims

ANTHOLOGY: THE 100 BEST N.Y./S.F. POETS

Two flourish. And a few may bud. But oh
That stench of the ninety-odd! We're grateful, though:
There's need of much manure where roses grow.

John Frederick Nims

ORIENTATING MR. BLANK

This will be your office, Mr. Blank,
While you remain attached to the Poetry
Division of the Department of Mediocrity.
Prose is down the hall, but we *all* work together—
Except for the two snobs upstairs in Innovation,
Who pretty much stick to themselves.

Now as to categories: Gays are by themselves,
In this drawer. Women who fill in their name blank
With "Ms." go in the Minority file (Drubb's innovation).
Don't file all the drug abusers under Nature Poetry.
Some are Deep Image; others get lumped, together
With younger academics, into regions. Mediocrity

Is *not* randomly distributed. True mediocrity,
Like genius, aggregates into nodes. By themselves
A dozen mediocrities amount to nothing, but put them
      together
And you have a department. You laugh, Mr. Blank,
But I am always serious when I speak of poetry.
What's New Under the Sun? as Mailer wrote, and
      innovation

Isn't the answer! The only *genuine* innovation
In the arts has been the belated recognition accorded
      mediocrity.
By forming poets into Schools and Offices of Poetry,
By helping them most generously to help themselves,
By encouraging their application to all forms of
      application blank,
They're made to learn that only by colluding together

Can poets obtain the object of money. Together-
Ness! "One Tribe, One Wall"—that was the first
        innovation
Of burghers in their boroughs, and now, Mr. Blank,
It is the last. Artists now see in their *united* mediocrity
A means toward the Golden Mean, and in themselves
A collective force for forming—and *re*-forming poetry

Into a once-more-*useful* social institution. Poetry
Is no longer the mere serial stringing-together
Of *aperçus* into prosodic masses, those masses themselves
To be collected in a book—even such a book as *The
        Innovation
Sheaves* (on which, by the by, I wrote my dissertation,
        "Mediocrity
In the work of Ezra Pound")! Well, Mr. Blank,

I hope that you and Mrs. Blank can come to our Poetry
Day Raffle. If not, Mediocrity often has a little
        get-together.
Usually *without* that pair from Innovation. They stick to
        themselves.

                                            Tom Disch

HOW I FLUNKED MY POETRY WRITING CLASS

Our dog used to crawl inside the refrigerator,
not in front where the food is,
but in back, with motor and electricity.
He was just a pup, no bigger than
two good hands cupped together.

Maybe once a week he'd crawl in
back there, and we'd be hollering for hours
before that dog crawled out again.
Course I was pretty small myself in those days.

Something happened to that dog,
but my poetry teacher says I'm not
supposed to write those kinds of poems,
so I wrote this:

One day my poetry teacher
was crossing our street when a big old car
squashed him flatter'n the cushion
under Aunt Matilda's rear end.
The car didn't even
slow down much.

We picked him up off the street
and buried him in the ground.

Jon Daunt

EDITOR'S DREAM
(a cover letter)

Hi. To begin on a personal note, I began
doing an in-depth study of ballroom dancing
and went on to audit a course by Northrop Frye.
I am assistant to the Director of Present Tense
Science Fiction Club and have appeared
mainly in *Hysteria* (three poems!).
Recently I spent a summer in Symbolism.
Since it is spring, I take my hat off
to you, and whatever else is necessary,
offering you and your fine Company
my First North American Serial Rights.
I do know a lot about rights,
should you decide to reproduce any part
of my "Elegy To An Elderly Lilac" (28 lines,
written age 32) without consent.
This poem, I might add, is my own work.
Not someone else's. I could be
what you've been looking for.
Enclosed are all my poems from the past
three years. Eagerly yours,

Katherine Soniat

DISCLAIMER

This poem, when written, contained 20 lines.
It is packaged according to weight, not length.
Some settling may have occurred due to handling,
or editing or last minute rewriting.

Joel Ferree

MY MUSE

My muse keeps irregular hours
Her name is Anthea which is a flower in Greece
It's obvious that she doesn't sit by her phone waiting for
    my calls
Don't call me, she says, I'll call you
And she calls at the most inconvenient hours, like 3 AM
    in the middle of the night
That seems to be a favorite time for her
Like when she might be getting home from a night on
    the town with some other poet
Naturally she doesn't tell me anything about him but I
    have my suspicions
If it turned out to be Howard Moss I would shoot her
But that really isn't likely because . . . well I won't say it
    . . . de mortuis in cerebro arteque nihil nisi
    bonum
She calls in the middle of the night a lot, it's like the old
    long distance operator before Ma Bell
    computerized
One ring then a little wait then three rings, I can always
    tell it's her
Anyway who else is going to call in the middle of the
    night
Unless it's Gregory Corso when he's been drinking
The last time Gregory called it was to ask me if I would
    leave him my teeth in my will
So she calls about 3 AM usually, my muse does
I have to keep a pencil and yellow pad handy to be ready
    for her
And sometimes she talks so fast I can't get it all down
    before she hangs up
It's inconvenient

But I'm loyal, we've been together, if you can call it that,
       for a long time
I suppose there are a lot of unemployed muses around on
       Helikon these days but I'm loyal, call me
       Philemon but she sure isn't Baucis
After she's called and I've written down her message I'm
       all keyed up and usually have to take half a valium
       to get back to sleep
I wish she would keep store hours
I wish I could call her and not have to wait for her to call
       me
But you know how muses are
I guess that's why old poets always had invocations to
       their muses at the start of their long poems
They were apple polishing, trying to keep their muse in
       line to get better service.

James Laughlin

LITMUS

To tell good poets I have this simple test:
To read their work stirs me to write my best.
Great poets are rather different. The latter
Suggest to me that I forget the matter.

F. C. Rosenberger

DIVIDENDS

Money is a kind of poetry—
Advice our great Assurer Stevens shared.
Yet who'd discount the statement, undeclared,
That *Poetry's a kind of money?*—since
The poem, whose returns, though nonfinancial,
Are active on the bourse of spirit, mints
All our common bonds as transubstantial
Coin, and puts our small change on the Real
Estate we'd hold in its entirety.
Straight from the ticker with investor's zeal
Imagination banks on poetry:
Experience laid by accrues interest,
At what per cent, we—whose security
Is balanced in such books—could scarce have guessed.

Daniel Hoffman

WOMAN POET

It's not easy—washing out poems
And writing underwear at the same time.

Carolyn Kizer

FAME

When fame comes you won't be able to use it.
The reward is new women, but you will have stopped
sleeping around. The reward is a certain amount
of cash, but you'll have lost all interest
in spending it, nor will you be able to find
those whom you'd enjoy spending it on. In a sense
they don't really exist. The reward is
having your name mentioned more,
but of what value a nose itching
in a foreign place, say walking past
hibiscus trees where red blooms sit
even on the low branches, or in
a barber's chair where the grey
clipped hair falls on your famous lap,
and what matters anything at all
in the magazines you do not read,
the cocktail party babble you always
fled from even when invited.

David Ray

A NOTE ON THE TYPE

This book was typed in 12 oz. Blue Ribbon,
a brew taken directly from the formula thought
to have been made by the Dutchman Anton Platz,
who was practicing his art in Leipzig during
the years 1668-1697. However, it has been
conclusively demonstrated that it is actually
the work of Nicholas Schiltz (1652-1768), an
obese Hungarian, who most probably learned his
trade from the master Dutch brewer Dick Yuengling.
This work is an excellent example of the influence
Dutch masters had on later brewers such as
Gunther, Kruger, Ballantine, Sterling and of course
Falstaff. It was from their work that Martin Lovell
Blue Ribbon developed his own incomparable pilsner.

Stephen E. Smith

7

THE IRAQIS ARE IN IRAQ &
THE IROQUOIS ARE IN NEW YORK

The Iraqis
Don't annoy
The Iroquois,
Iroquois
Don't tease
The Iraqis
If you wish
Peace to start,
Keep everybody
Far apart.

Louis Phillips

BEESTIRRINGS

How doth the busy little bee
  Throw nations into schism?
By dint of the fecundity
  Of his metabolism!

The Yellow Rain that sore beset
  Afghanistan and Laos
At first seemed proof the Soviet
  Was spreading instant chaos,

But now the rain has been researched
  And scientific theses
Imply that it was just besmirched
  By bees emitting feces.

The busy bee must be contained
  Before the crops grow riper:
His Queen must get him toilet trained
  Or make him wear a diaper.

Felicia Lamport

THE YEAR TO WATCH

I predict the world will be
A place of peace and plenty
When heads of state see eye to eye—
Perhaps in 2020?

Ned Pastor

ROMANTIC PIG

Pretend there's alternatives.
The second brother
declines the bunker,

beats the bloody system.
In his home-made boat
he's fishing off Bimini,

leaner than most, but grinning.
Pretend there's
no winning or losing

off Bimini.
No Three Little Fish.
No Big Bad Pig.

Bonnie Jacobson

HISTORY AMUSES ITSELF

"A circle amuses itself."

Hans Arp

I want to draw: squiggles.
They focus into engravings of Sukarno,
Triple-deckers in Djakarta, coffee plantation owners.
I draw a Dutch ocean liner colliding with an underground
      rock.
Next panel it capsizes, next panel it slips under the
      water.

This happens off the coast of Borneo.
An Indonesian girl shakes her skirt,
Mountains rumba.
I draw the Dutch scholars of Indonesian History,
Taking coffee and nipping donuts on the Presidential
      palace porch.
Their big conference starts tomorrow.
They seem to wish they could be up in their hotel rooms,
Clutching big green bottles of 7-Up as they recover from
      jet lag.
Respect for history is slipping on a banana peel.

Kirby Olson

STILL SMALL VOICE

When I think of my faithful wife of many years
who is still charming
and has a good job,
of my three beautiful daughters
who are doing well in college,
of how I am respected at work,
of how my writing is getting published,
of the real estate to which I hold title,
including several saleable parcels
and a number of large trees,
of the money in the bank
I'll probably never spend,
sometimes I have a sense of doom.

Richard Moore

POPCORN

It seems so right to sit here eating some popcorn,
dipping out handfuls of gentle white explosions,
relishing the contrast between cold bourbon and warm
       salt,
at ease with the world here within this ring of lamplight,
not yet satisfied but certainly no longer hungry,
selecting a last few morsels from among the old maids.

Another nice contrast: the small smooth brown old maids
against the white puffed irregularity of the popcorn.
When they're all that's left I'm glad I'm not hungry—
taut they are, swollen, threatening small explosions,
but held in by the comfortable circle of lamplight,
and the bowl, and pacified by fine small jewels of salt.

Of course, one of you is bound to observe that so much
       salt
provokes high blood pressure, and that hard old maids
break teeth, that scarce fuels burned to make my
       lamplight
and were processed into fertilizer to grow the popcorn.
While I indulge myself, the population explosion
booms: my pleasure against the misery of the truly
       hungry.

Of course, about now some woman among you's hungry
for justice, every word I say rubbing coarse salt
into an old wound, on the verge of a real explosion
at my thoughtless endorsement of the phrase "old maid":
a long history of exploitation trivialized by popcorn,
suffering in the shadows beyond the comfy male
       lamplight.

To say nothing of that definitive intense lamplight
ready to gather in its expanding ring both hungry
and fed, ready to shadow under clouds like monster
        popcorn
all of us, ready when we're finally sick of futile SALT
talks to gather us by handfuls, young, old, maids
and men, dissolving all contrast in one ghastly explosion.

All right, all right: I'll try to stop the explosion,
illuminate that darkness there beyond my lamplight.
But don't the rest of you in contrast sit there like old
        maids:
get out there, heal the sick, clothe the naked, feed the
        hungry,
battle indifference and injustice and discrimination,
        assault
fear, persuade the Others to trade guns for buttered
        popcorn.

First, though, we old maids and health freaks are a bit
        hungry.
Gathering forces by lamplight, even the very best, the salt
of the earth's explosion, can use the sustenance of a little
        popcorn.

David Evett

VACILLATION

Some people think the world is round.
I think that this idea is sound.
While others think that it is flat.
I think there's nothing wrong in that!

Richard J. Vaules, Jr.

CUSTARD'S LAST STAND

A bunch of Indians
ate up all the ice cream
in Crow Agency, Montana.

James Preston

DO NOT DISTURB

". . . An admission by his deputy
chief of staff, Michael K. Deaver, . . .
that Mr. Reagan sometimes naps
during cabinet meetings . . ."

Our leader sleeps. Let none that slumber break;
His mind more active now than when awake.

Bruce Bennett

WHO ELSE IS SLEEPING IN MY BED?

"I liked it better when the the actors kept their clothes on."

—Ronald Reagan

Each time I give a private screening
I find the movie quite demeaning.
The actors are profane and crude
And sleep together in the nude.
Bring back the days when we had faces
And love was merely chaste embraces.
Then one could win it for the Gipper
And never be a skinny dipper.
A kilt might show a Hasty Heart
But kept well hid the private part.
Even in King's Row the best of me
Was all you saw, not the rest of me.
Bedtime for Bonzo I most adore:
I kept one foot upon the floor.

Edward Watkins

LET'S HEAR IT FOR CONGRESS

Hollywood gives Oscars,
Broadway gives Tonys,
TV gives Emmys
To ballyhooed cronies.
Since Adland gives Andys
And Music gives Grammys,
Is it time for Congress
To give Uncle Sammys?

Ned Pastor

BALLAD OF THE NATIONAL RIFLE ASSOCIATION

"For the greatest in shooting satisfaction . . ."
—Handgun ad.

Pistol, small arm, handgun, gun,
Trooper, Trailsman, Frontier Scout,
Smith & Wesson, Remington,
Combat, Cobra, Knockabout;
Browning, Sheridan, Colt Snap-Out,
Single-six and Double-action,
"Top performance," "Super clout,"
Give you shooting satisfaction.

Pistol, short arm, peter, prick,
Rod, avenger, redmeat, dong;
Johnny, joystick, reamer, dick,
Dummy, fixer, hicky, prong,
Swinging sirloin two feet long,
Have a similar attraction:
Every boy can be King Kong
With a shooting satisfaction.

Pistol-heist her, hunt her down,
Line her up and ream her right;
Ride her home, get off your gun,
Shag her, shoot her up tonight;
Jump her, hump her out of sight,
Whang her, bang her, get your action,
Fill her full of dynamite
For your shooting satisfaction.

Pistol Po-lice, save your pity
For the dirty rotten hood;
Gun him down in Inner City

Like they do in Hollywood;
Save your daughter's maidenhood
And pulverize the putrefaction:
Blast him, buddy, blast him good!
For your shooting satisfaction.

Pistol Pentheus, git yer maw
Afore she tears you limb from limb;
Beat yer pappy to the draw
And incidentally get *him*
The sonovabitch who wants yer skin
To add it to his rug collection;
Chop the Copper, Jungle Jim!
Fer yer shootin' satisfaction.

Pistol Patriot, shoot your wad,
The world, the moon, your mouth, your brother;
Build Jerusalem, by God,
Winging rockets at each other;
Love your country like a mother,
Love your enemy dog-fashion,
Love your neighbor till he smother
In your shooting satisfaction.

Envoy

Pistol Pirate, cool tycoon,
Do us all a benefaction:
Go take a flying leap at the moon
For *our* shooting satisfaction!

Scott Bates

ON WELFARE

We have two ways to aid the poor
Down here in Jackson City:
A white-draped basket at the door;
A similar committee.

William Wilborn

HOG ROAST

If the town celebrates
his roasting
it's their right. He's their hog.
He's pork now.

His life in the mash has gone sour.
The bad fairy presides
over his crispy feet.
The prodigal has come back

and does not need
such company.
Now the fire licks this one all over.
Now the fire is giving its best

hog massage.
Corn-fed hog is sweet.
But sweet as a dog
to the prodigal

he's pork now.
And he cannot know better next time.
He cannot cry to the prodigal:
You, little one, shod

in your doubts,
run along to your gorgeous friends!
He cannot cry:
Let me see your back!

He's pork now.
So we can kiss—if we want—
his blarney lips.
So? So we're home,

barely edible,
lonely with the whole town.
So no one's lonely in hog heaven.
No one's got cooked feet.

Lee Upton

KONG INCOGNITO

The secret is to blend in, choose neutral
colors in patterns that break up the silhouette,
and, in my case, slouch a little, avoid vertical
stripes, and wear dark glasses. Even when
everything else is right, my eyes can betray me.
And the voice, keep it high in the throat
like this: "eeeeeee," being careful to always
say average things. For instance, when greeted,
say, "I am fine. Where are you?" or "Yes,
the weather today is free of cats and dogs.
My temperature is typical." When driving
in heavy traffic, say, "Up yours, motherfucker."
This is what average people say to one another
when a foreigner's not around and they don't
have to shoot him before asking any questions.

William Trowbridge

NEWTON WAS A NEURO FROM NEW ROCHELLE

Newton was a neuro from New Rochelle:
He had the habit of reading *Babbitt*
To a rabbit named Nelle.
Newton had obsessions: he liked to pee
In little thimbles
He bought at Gimbel's;
Did it constantly.
Newton had a trauma,
Got it from his mama,
A woman who disordered many lives.

In the family water closet
She used to deposit
Objects like cleavers and knives.
Newton's new neuroses are always swell:
His current fear is
The fear of mirrors
In chocolate bar machines—
It's hell
To be Newton the neuro from New Rochelle.

Newton's first obsession
Centered on a Hessian
Who took Newton, late one evening, to a drag.
There he stood upon a table,
Exposed a large, unsightly navel
And waved the American flag.
Newton's new neuroses, etc. . . . .

*Weldon Kees**

*

"Weldon," said Kenneth Rexroth, "affected the personality, appearance and behavior of a Canadian Air Force ace playing a twenties-style piano, singing in a jazz bass, and remembering all the lyrics."

Janet Richards, *Common Soldiers*

Written during the war years and published here for the first time, "Newton Was a Neuro" is a song that Kees may have performed for friends and strangers alike at Cedar Tavern, or some other haunt where the jukebox had not yet replaced the upright.

—James Reidel

AFTER BAUDELAIRE

Sometimes I am bored in America
Where no one resembles Voltaire.

Carolyn Kizer

NOTES ON A LONG-STANDING SOCIAL AND/OR CIVIC PHENOMENON

Committee meetings, if held at all,
Are sometimes haphazard, and frequently small,
For most of the members are out when you call.
("Well, nobody told *me* about it!")

The session is scheduled weeks in advance
In hopes that some members who happen, by chance,
To notice the notice will give it a glance.
("Are you sure that I got one? I doubt it!")

The meeting is always a little bit late.
("Did you say seven-thirty? I thought you said eight!")
And too often, no matter what's on the slate,
It turns out to be a pure pastime:

Though the meeting is called to discuss this and that,
The members end up merely having a chat.
Can they help it if they don't know where they're at?
They're the ones who were absent the last time!

Hallie Hodgson

APARTMENT HUNTING

12 Sept. 1978

While ordinarily I quite admire the wolves
With whom I am acquainted—their sharp eyes,
Bright teeth, and invariable good humour—
I find it disconcerting, as a rabbit,
To learn that they're in charge
Of the Department of Safety and Burrows.

Tom Disch

SOCIETY

I travelled in society.
They all put mint in their iced tea.
The women clip their sentences.
The men look upward when they pee.

Joan Halperin

GENUS ENVY

I bet every white lab mouse in America
wishes it were a least tern, snail darter, or
even a humpback whale.

Sheila Seiler

LITTERGY

Leaves and dews
naturally as the
light of stars,
fall.
    Budweiser,
too, and empties
lofted out of
midnight cars.

This bank of
earth, this
day and night
depository.

Ernest Kroll

TRUE ROMANCE

Ten a.m. Whistle of doves' wings.
The young ones flying relay
orchard to garage to guava tree.
I'm grading essays. It must be Wednesday.
Intrusion of the telephone. "Hello.
"My name is Robert." Salesman
fake. Someone who wants to please, no
who wants me to believe he wants to please.
The only Robert I know is a night student,
fond of words like Realistic Constructs,
Congruent Goals, Interfacing with Our Shifting
        Parameters,
whose senior thesis, I'm beginning to believe, is
Creative Excuses for Delaying the Assigned Paper.

This Robert is a machine.
Wants to give me a Citicorp Visa card.
"Already we've established $5000 line-of-credit
on your name alone." He's confident he can satisfy
all my questions—Why
do I call this bacon-brained arrangement
of wires and flashing lights, *he*?
I've heard this voice before, bland, reasonable,
wants me to say *yes*, to believe
there's nothing in it for him.
Robert is a good listener, nods his head, smiles,
sips his wine, Almaden light chablis,
always buckles his seat belt,
flosses daily.
He likes the lights out when we make love.
Afterwards he doesn't want to talk.
When I leave him I want to do crazy things,
like open all the windows and play Beethoven's 9th
at full volume, or pedal a fifteen-speed bike ten miles
            uphill,
the long curving hill over the Santa Cruz mountains,
then let the steep downhill take me out of control
to the beach, the breakers crashing in at high tide.
I want to startle him, make him stammer,
say something ungrammatical. I want to hear Missouri
or Texas or the Bronx in his voice.
A real place.
A real person who once was a child.
I hang up quietly, knowing
he will notate my response in the appropriate column,
that already he's forgotten my name, already dialing
another number. "Hello, my name is Robert."

Sally Croft

AGE OF REASON

Computers will be truly smart
When they can vent their spleens
By practicing the human art
Of kicking dumb machines.

Mary Mobilia

DATA MATTER

I used to feel neuter
About the computer.
Its influence then, though, was scanty.
But now its vast powers
Are transcending ours,
It makes us cry "uncle." I'm ANTI!

Maureen Cannon

COM-GLITCH I

I keyed a number
on the phone
but didn't get a ring.

The operator
answered and
I got a dingaling.

Noa Spears

GHOSTS

Although I don't believe in ghosts,
I keep hoping that I'll see one.
For, if they really do exist,
Then, maybe, someday I'll be one.

John A. Haliburton

SIXSOME

Wacky, oracular
JOHN THE APOCALYPT
Gave us a glimpse of the
Heavenly State,
Saw with precision his
Mystical vision was
Paradisiacal
(Something he ate?)

*

Vermin exterminate
PIPER OF HAMELIN
Handled removals of
Pests from the town;
Broadening service to
Cover the kiddies brought
Musicologically
Lasting renown.

*

Arrogant paragon
KATHARINE OF ARAGON
Hitched onto Henry's her
Marital star;
Thinking how blessed he was,
Hank never guessed she was
Gynecologically
Way below Parr.

*

Mistress-distressable
MADAME DE POMPADOUR
Sported a wig that was
Formally gay,

Happily whored to be—
Would've adored to be—
Plenipotentially
Queen for a day.

*

Floral, deplorable
LITTLE LORD FAUNTLEROY
Lavished on mater his
Filial goo;
Hair all acurl, he was
Heir to an earl and too
Superabundantly
Good to be true.

*

Purple, puerperal
PRINCESS VICTORIA,
Landing a consort who
Honestly cares,
Takes to the royal life,
Makes him a loyal wife—
Uninterruptedly
Gives herself heirs.

C. Webster Wheelock

EPITAPH

I hereby leave my worldly goods
to all deserving brotherhoods;
and if this does not suit the lads,
they're welcome to my worldly bads.

Michael Braude

THE URN

The cold urn signifies that Nonnie never
back across the NaCl H2O
shall venture nor the fardeled spaniel persever
with his lemon liquid eye bones to bestow:
the old consul has deserved well of the state
and is translated into winter quarters
in cisalpine Gaul who what with her deckled borders
and all is some eclectic numinous broad
(polemics billow forth and plays are written
—the urn's the province of the orthopod)
comfortable and fecund and ornate
yet chafed in the gizzard by Armorican Britain.
    Chalk one up for the caterpillars of
    the commonwealth and their parataxis, love.

Caroline Knox

TOPPING OFF

Now of my three score years and ten
sixty-nine won't come again.
And take from seventy years all that—
I think I'll buy a new spring hat.

Emily Otis

FRUSTRATION

I don't know whether to play it safe
Or just live like I always do.
It's a lot more fun like I always do
But I don't want to finish before I'm through.

Jack V. Adler

ONE HAMBURGER, PLAIN

Hold the catsup,
Skip the pickle;
My stomach's grouchy,
Nervous, fickle.

I'll have to coddle it,
Not glut it.
And don't mention mustard—
I just can't cut it.

Margaret Blaker

FABLE

When I was young and pretty
I had a little kitty.
Now that I'm old and fat,
I find I've got a cat.

Hubert E. Hix

WHEN JOINTS ARE OUT OF JOINT

I'm sometimes of a mind to curse a
Parched and malperforming bursa:
But when I do, it's vice versa!

Charles Lee

A MODEL PRISON

Benign Tumors Of the Heart Were Killers Once
—headline in *The New York Times*

Repentant now, they fill the cells
With Kyries and rebel yells.
"Death No More" in blood is scrawled
Across the cafeteria walls.
Into their arms they've carved paired hearts,
And other lost or stolen arts
Revive in shops that hum like hives.
Observing this, we spare their lives.

Tom Disch

EYE-CATCHING

Aerobic dancing
Jazzercise
I love to watch
It strengthens
My eyes.

Bill Delaney

SLIMERICK

A lady who slendered too madly
Regarded her silhouette sadly,
   For the pounds that she lost
   At such strenuous cost
Were from right where she needed 'em badly.

Paul Humphrey

THE ABC OF AEROBICS

Air seeps through alleys and our diaphragms
balloon blackly with this mix of
carbon monoxide and the thousand corrosives a city
doles out free to its constituents;
everyone's jogging through Edgemont Park,
frightened by death and fatty tissue,
gasping at the maximal heart rate,
hoping to outlive all the others streaming
in the lanes like lemmings lurching toward their last
jump. I join in despair
knowing my arteries jammed with
lint and tobacco, lard and bourbon—my
medical history a noxious marsh:
newts and moles slink through the sodden veins,
owls hoot in the lungs' dark branches;
probably I shall keel off the john like
queer Uncle George and lie on the bathroom floor
raging about Shirley Clark, my true love in
seventh grade, God bless her wherever she lives
tied to that turkey who hugely
undervalues the beauty of her tiny earlobes, one
view of which (either one: they are both perfect)
would add years to my life and I could skip these
x-rays, turn in my insurance card, and trade
yoga and treadmills and jogging and zen and
zucchini for drinking and dreaming of her, breathing hard.

Peter Meinke

IN MEDIAS RES

His waist
like the plot
thickens, wedding
pants now breathtaking,
belt no longer the cinch
it once was, belly's cambium
expanding to match each birthday,
his body a wad of anonymous tissue
swung in the same centrifuge of years
that separates a house from its foundation,
undermining sidewalks grim with joggers
and loose-filled graves and families
and stars collapsing on themselves,
no preservation society capable
of plugging entropy's dike,
under his zipper's sneer
a belly hibernation–
soft, ready for
the kill.

Michael McFee

LIGHT WOMAN SPEAK WITH FORKED TONGUE

Her compliments
Were never meant to flatter,
Who says, "You're looking well,"
But means, "You're getting fatter."

Ruth Stewart Schenley

• 263

THE IRONY OF BEING DIFFERENT

The rebels of the world we see
  Define their eccentricity
By wearing clothes and styling hair
  Designed to make us stop and stare.
The irony in what they do
  Is, many others will then too
Appear in this outlandish way,
  And we'll be odd instead of they.

Richard J. Vaules, Jr.

BALD EGO

Stunning bird.
Proud. Erect.

Laid alone.
Hatched high.

Hungry. Brave.
Unflockable.

Feed him.
Watch him soar.

Charles Ghigna

NEWTON DRUNK

His fingers find their grip.
He ascends. "Isaac? Are you ill?"
"Ill, beloved." Eyes closed,

the world floats, suspends him; he
starts awake. Asleep and standing!
　　　　The chamber pot
rings like a distant wedding.
Eased, he finds the bedpost.
He holds tight. Who has his
strength of will, his power of
following the obvious?

He will not fall.

Michael Cadnum

THE GIG AT POWELL'S MILL

Dark spilled on Powell's mill,
and drunk on brutal hootch
sat Isaac Boone. His pooch
sniffed at the mud-marsh logs
as low tromboning frogs
droned on at them until
old Isaac, stewed, stood up.
His flashlight froze the pack.
A hundred eyes stared back,
the frogs as big as fists.
Ike saw the soloists'
sober glares, and the pup,
stiff in a tripod stance,
saw them too, but barked once,
enough to spook the runts,
who nonchalantly sank
deep off the millpond bank.
Ike did a little dance
and howled at the moon,
then kicked the dog and swore,
"What the hell you good for?!"
when two frogs, blind or mad,
launched off a lily pad,
their destination: Boone,
and crashed against his crotch,
fell, squirming in the mud.
As if to right the wrong,
Ike spiked the rusted prong
down hard. The loaded blow
hit home—his middle toe!
His boot filled up with blood.
His blood filled up with swill
of Mississippi Scotch,

he belched, bellowed a long
ungodly banshee song
until three Powell boys,
hearing the inhuman noise,
crept on down to the mill.
Moaning in the moon-thick
light, he took another swig,
sprawled, skewered on the gig.
The boys spoke up, "You dead,
Mister?" "Damn near," he said.
"That dog ain't worth a lick."

J. Patrick Lewis

BOOZE

To deprive me
I think
Would drive me
To drink.

Edmund Conti

THE BATTLE OF MULDOON'S

What are you lily-livered rascals at?
Just because Casey's down you're running off?
You cannot be such little girls as that.

Too bad if one guy's got a baseball bat.
It's when fists fail that bellies must be tough.
What are you lily-livered rascals at?

This isn't just some private household spat.
Our Casey's down. Now isn't that enough?
You cannot be such little girls as that,

to leave him on the floor alone. You sat
with him tonight and drank his drinking stuff.
What are you lily-livered rascals at,

thinking that you can quick put on your hat
and take your leave with just a nervous cough?
You cannot be such little girls as that.

Hell swallow every damn ungrateful rat
that scurries off when things start getting rough.
What are you lily-livered rascals at?
You cannot be such little girls as that.

Tom Riley

MCALISTAIR'S FORMULA FOR GETTING
KANGAROOS TO FALL ASLEEP ON STAIRCASES

First
you've got to get them
drunk on highballs, then
lead them quietly (a scarf
tied gently around the snout
will dampen the
hiccoughs) to the homes
or apartment houses
or isolated little flats
of the people you want to scare
to screaming hell
at eight o'clock the next morning.

Katharyn Machan Aal

REVENGE

I think of my enemies
and, in a moment of weakness,
summon the forces of Imperial Japan.

Later I will regret this,
but now it is too late to stop them,
for having breakfasted

on black tea, rice, and pickles,
having listened to a fiery speech
by Foreign Minister Matsuoka,

the celebrated Talking Machine,
Mr. 50,000 Words, they move forward,
led by the Nine Young Men of Niigata,

who were so willing to die
that they sent their own nine fingers
in a jar of alcohol.

There are hundreds of soldiers now,
each wearing the hachimaki headband
and the belt into which his mother

has woven a thousand prayers
for good luck and a good fight.
At first they are joking,

saying "Don't miss the bus!"
and jostling each other,
but before long their eyes are bright

and they are shouting "Sleep on kindling,
lick gall!" and "We must have courage
to do extraordinary things—

like jumping, with eyes closed,
off the verandah of the Kiyomizu Temple!"
Now they are running

in full banzai formation,
tens of thousands of khaki-clad men
flashing bayonets, swords, battle flags,

screaming "Punishment of Heaven!"
or simply "Wah! Charge!"
as the Kaiten human torpedoes

tunnel through the azaleas
and, overhead, the Iron Typhoon!
the Heavenly Wind!

the White Chrysanthemum bombers
falling, falling, as I urge them on
in my cocked hat, plumes, braids,

decorations, my gold-headed cane
pounding the ground,
my voice rising shrilly

in a jackhammer stutter,
screaming Suck on this,
you sons of b-bitches, you bastards!

David Kirby

PRO TEMPORE

(to our seven-foot sophomores)

Godspeed, with prayers:
Nunc Dimittis
To the players
Who dunk and quit us.

Edmund Conti

THE COMPETITION BLUES

When I'm on the range
My swing is precise;
So why, on the course,
Do I tend to slice?

As soon as I'm sure
My woods are down pat,
How come, in a match,
I hit 'em all fat?

Each chip I rehearse
Runs straight to the pin;
In play, it takes three
To get up and in!

"Practice makes perfect!"
The pros all decree;
But why does it work
For them and not me?

Ned Pastor

PASTORAL

On the green's verge stands a cottage;
   Red its roof and white its walls.
Within, a lady in her dotage
   Sells admissions, tees, and balls.

Her legend's ancient, and is tethered
   To a little picket fence,
And may be read there, somewhat weathered:
   Public GOLF *Links* 80¢.

Above her hardened head hang hardened
   Stroboscopic ikons of
Sammy Snead and Harvie Ward and
   Dr. Cary Middlecoff.

Her candies are for her nibble.
   Stout and shawled and stolid, she
Is like a pre-ecstatic sibyl,
   Chewing something silently.

A sibyl? Nay, she's Lethe's daughter,
   Guarding till the end of time
Springs of refrigerated water
   Cooling lemon pop, and lime.

Those who dare to pass beyond her
   Sink into forgetfulness
Beneath her curse and ever wander
   Through the bunkers of distress.

John Updike

ACKNOWLEDGMENTS

All poems not listed hereunder are printed in *Light Year '86* for the first time; copyright remains vested in the poets. The following poems, previously copyrighted, are reprinted by permission of their authors or as otherwise indicated.

W. H. Auden. "Ode" and "Ribald Limericks": © 1984 by the Estate of W. H. Auden. Reprinted by permission of Edward Mendelson. The limericks are from the versions given in Dorothy Farnan's *Auden in Love*.

Jean Balderston. "Battlegrounds": © 1984 by Jean Balderston. First appeared in *The Little Magazine*.

Robert Bess. "Attila the Hen": © 1985 by Robert Bess. First appeared in *Artemis*.

Maureen Cannon. "Staying Power": © 1981 by Maureen Cannon. First appeared in *The Saturday Evening Post*. "Data Matter": © 1973 by Maureen Cannon. First appeared in *American Journal of Nursing*.

Sally Croft. "Home-Baked Bread": © 1981 by Sally Croft. First appeared in *Tar River Poetry*.

Alma Denny. "The Fallen Thumbtack": © 1949 by Alma Denny. First appeared in *The American Legion Magazine*.

Tom Disch. "Marking Time": © 1984 by Tom Disch. First appeared in *Lake Street Review*. "Entropic Villanelle" and "Working for a Tan": © 1984 by Tom Disch. Both first appeared in *Poetry*. "Orientating Mr. Blank": © 1984 by Tom Disch. First appeared in *Paris Review*. "Apartment Hunting": © 1984 by Tom Disch. Reprinted from *Here I Am, There You Are, Where Were We*, Hutchinson's, UK, 1984. "A Model Prison": © 1984 by Tom Disch. First appeared in *Amazing/Fantastic*.

Thomas Emery. "Capre Diem": © 1983 by Thomas Emery. First appeared in *Scholia Satyrica*.

Gene Fehler. "If A. E. Housman Had Tried to Hit Big League Pitching": © 1984 by Gene Fehler. First appeared in *Capper's Weekly*. "If Robert Frost Managed the Yankees": © 1984 by Gene Fehler. First appeared in *Spitball*.

Robert N. Feinstein. "Wrong Turnings": © 1983 by Robert N. Feinstein. First appeared in *The Lyric*.

Barbara Goldberg. "Song While Arranging Jasmine and Jewelweed": © 1983 by Barbara Goldberg. First appeared in *Tendril*.

Ray Griffith. "Rooms": © 1984 by Ray Griffith. First appeared in *Windfall*.

John A. Haliburton. "Ghosts": © 1979 by John A. Haliburton. First appeared in *Kenning View*.

Donald Hall. The second stanza of "A 3rd Stanza for Dr. Johnson & Donald Hall": © 1955 by Donald Hall as "A Second Stanza for Dr. Johnson." Reprinted from *Exiles and Marriages*.

Louis Hasley. "Oh, Lord, Tennyson": © 1972 by Louis Hasley. First appeared in *The CEA Critic*. "The Jinky Junk": © 1967 by Louis Hasley. First appeared in *The Leprechaun* (Notre Dame). "Love in the Rough": © 1982 by Louis Hasley. First appeared in "Action Line," *South Bend Tribune*.

William Hathaway. "Oh, Oh": © 1982 by William Hathaway. First appeared in *Cincinnati Poetry Review*.

Dorothy Heller. "Move Over, Uri Geller": © 1985 by Dorothy Heller. First appeared in *Cat Fancy*.

Hallie Hodgson. "Notes on a Long-Standing Social and/or Civic Phenomenon": © 1985 by Hallie Schraeger. First appeared in *The Outlook*, Monmouth College.

Barbara D. Holender "Lot's Wife": © 1982 by Barbara D. Holender. First appeared in *Escarpment*.

Paul Humphrey. "Slimerick": © 1983 by Paul Humphrey. First appeared in *Pulpsmith*.

Bonnie Jacobson. "Romantic Pig": © 1985 by Bonnie Jacobson. First appeared in *Negative Capability*.

Weldon Kees. "Newton Was a Neuro from New Rochelle": © 1985 by the Estate of Weldon Kees.

Caroline Knox. "The House Party": © 1984 by Caroline Knox. Reprinted from *The House Party* by permission of the University of Georgia Press.

Felicia Lamport. "Eggomania": © 1983 by Felicia Lamport. Reprinted from *Light Metres*. "Sea

INDEX OF POETS